C000164507

Your Space

Student's Book 3

Martyn Hobbs and Julia Starr Keddle

CAMBRIDGE
UNIVERSITY PRESS

CAMBRIDGE
UNIVERSITY PRESS

University Printing House, Cambridge CB2 8BS, United Kingdom

Cambridge University Press is part of the University of Cambridge.

It furthers the University's mission by disseminating knowledge in the pursuit of education, learning and research at the highest international levels of excellence.

www.cambridge.org
Information on this title: www.cambridge.org/9780521729338

© Cambridge University Press 2012

This publication is in copyright. Subject to statutory exception and to the provisions of relevant collective licensing agreements, no reproduction of any part may take place without the written permission of Cambridge University Press.

First published 2012
5th printing 2014

Printed in Poland by Opolgraf

A catalogue record for this publication is available from the British Library

ISBN 978-0-521-72933-8 Student's Book, Level 3
ISBN 978-0-521-72934-5 Workbook with Audio CD, Level 3
ISBN 978-0-521-72935-2 Teacher's Book with Tests CD, Level 3
ISBN 978-0-521-72937-6 Class Audio CDs (3), Level 3

Cambridge University Press has no responsibility for the persistence or accuracy of URLs for external or third-party internet websites referred to in this publication, and does not guarantee that any content on such websites is, or will remain, accurate or appropriate. Information regarding prices, travel timetables, and other factual information given in this work is correct at the time of first printing but Cambridge University Press does not guarantee the accuracy of such information thereafter.

Contents

Functions	Skills		
Talking about the past	**Reading:** Understanding an article about New Year's Eve.	**Pronunciation** /əʊ/ /aʊ/	
	Listening: Understanding information about New Year's resolutions.	**Study skills** Chatting	
Talking about duties and rules	**Speaking:** Describing New Year's celebrations.		
	Writing: Writing your New Year's resolutions.		
Asking about rules			
Talking about the future	**Reading:** Understanding an article about city life in the future.	**Pronunciation** Syllables	
	Listening: Understanding students talking about life in the future.	**Study skills** Guessing meaning	
Talking about plans	**Speaking:** Discussing your opinions of life in the future.		
	Writing: Writing about your view of the future.		
Describing a picture			
Talking about experiences	**Reading:** Understanding a factfile about an activity award.	**Pronunciation** /h/	
Talking about duration	**Listening:** Understanding a radio programme about an activity award.	**Study skills** True/False questions	
	Speaking: Planning an adventure journey.		
Negotiating	**Writing:** Writing a description of your planned expedition.		
Talking about recent events	**Reading:** Understanding an article about Buy Nothing Day.	**Pronunciation** /θ/ /ð/	
Giving opinions	**Listening:** Understanding a questionnaire about shopping.	**Study skills** *wh-* questions	
	Speaking: Talking about your shopping habits.		
Buying clothes	**Writing:** Writing about your opinions on Buy Nothing Day.		
Talking about facts, results and conditions	**Reading:** Understanding an article about children's rights.	**Pronunciation** /w/ /v/	
Defining and explaining	**Listening:** Understanding information about the lives of three children.	**Study skills** Be prepared	
Joining information	**Speaking:** Talking about human rights.		
Going to the doctor's	**Writing:** Writing about things you like about your life.		

Contents

Functions	Skills	
Giving opinions Reporting	**Reading:** Understanding an article about film production. **Listening:** Understanding people talking about their jobs in film. **Speaking:** Talking about your future career. **Writing:** Writing a short text about your future career.	**Pronunciation** /uː/ /ʊ/ **Study skills** Getting the gist
Talking about films Reporting Taking messages		
Talking about imaginary situations Talking about politics Giving advice	**Reading:** Understanding an article about a school council. **Listening:** Understanding students talking about their concerns over social problems. **Speaking:** Talking about setting up a school council. **Writing:** Writing about social issues.	**Pronunciation** /ɪə/ /eə/ **Study skills** Paragraphs
Talking about processes Speaking and listening accurately Talking about feelings	**Reading:** Understanding a text about different ways of communicating. **Listening:** Understanding information about emotions. **Speaking:** Talking about different types of greetings. **Writing:** Writing a text about an emotion you have experienced.	**Pronunciation** /e/ /eɪ/ **Study skills** Using the internet
Talking about a city Talking about shopping centres and shopping Giving directions	**Reading:** Understanding a text about megacities. **Listening:** Understanding two students describing their cities. **Speaking:** Talking about a city in your own country. **Writing:** Writing a text about a city in your own country.	**Pronunciation** Rising and falling intonation **Study skills** Writing about a city
Talking about your family Fluency practice Saying goodbye	**Reading:** Understanding an article about the dancer Carlos Acosta. **Listening:** Understanding people talking about their lives. **Speaking:** Talking to the class about your life. **Writing:** Writing the beginning of a biography of someone you know.	**Pronunciation** /p/ /b/ **Study skills** Putting events in order

Grammar
past simple Ⓡ · past continuous Ⓡ ·
when / while

Functions
talking about the past

Vocabulary • Festivals and special days

1 Work in pairs. Think about a festival or special day.
Say what happens. Use the photos and words to help you.

On birthdays we give presents. We have a party and eat a special cake.

> wear   watch   give   go to   eat
> listen to   dance to   take part in

traditional music

special food

fireworks

church / mosque /
temple / synagogue

traditional costumes

presents

parades

Presentation

2 **Warm up** Look at the photos and captions on page 9. What jobs do the
friends have on the webzine?

3 Read the webzine on page 9. Write *N* (Nathan), *H* (Holly), *J* (Josh), or *S* (Samira).

Who…

1 celebrated a festival in Bangladesh?   `S`
2 went to a music festival?   ☐
3 went to New York?   ☐
4 crashed a bike?   ☐
5 played in the school football team?   ☐
6 went to school in a pair of slippers?   ☐
7 saw fireworks in London?   ☐
8 threw away a mobile phone?   ☐

4 Read *Language focus*. Find two more
sentences with *when* in the webzine on page 9.

> ### Language focus
>
> I noticed an interesting advert **while**
> I was riding my bike.
> We were putting up our tent **when** it
> started to rain.
> I was talking on my mobile **while**
> I was taking the rubbish out.

5 Complete the sentences with these verbs. Use the past simple or the past continuous.

> burn   hear   read   see   watch   happen   ~~walk~~   steal

1 He ___was walking___ down the road while he was sending a text message.
2 They were eating ice cream when they _____ their old teacher.
3 When the accident _____, I was chatting with my friends.
4 While we _____ TV, our dinner _____ in the oven.
5 The dog _____ my sandwich while I _____ a magazine.
6 I _____ the news while I was listening to the radio.

webzine

LATEST ISSUE

Meet the WEB CREW!
What's a webzine? It's a web magazine! And we create it. So read about us here.

NATHAN writer

WORST EVER MOMENT
I was playing in an inter-school football match when I took a penalty kick ... and I missed! We lost the match.

BEST EVER FESTIVAL
On New Year's Eve we were in London. We were standing near the London Eye at midnight when Big Ben struck twelve. Then we watched an awesome firework display.

HOLLY photographer and video operator

WORST EVER MOMENT
I noticed an interesting advert while I was riding my bike. I turned to look at it and I crashed into a tree! All my friends were watching.

BEST EVER FESTIVAL
We were in New York on St Patrick's Day. We watched an incredible parade. Thousands of people were wearing green costumes, playing Irish music and dancing traditional dances.

JOSH webzine designer and illustrator

WORST EVER MOMENT
One morning I was late and I forgot to put my shoes on. I went to school in my slippers!

BEST EVER FESTIVAL
My dad took me and my cousins to Glastonbury music festival. We were putting up our tent when it started to rain. So we watched the bands and danced in the rain!

SAMIRA technical expert (and occasional writer!)

WORST EVER MOMENT
I was talking on my mobile while I was taking the rubbish out. Then I threw my mobile in the rubbish bin by mistake!

BEST EVER FESTIVAL
In my family we celebrate a festival called Eid. One year we went to Bangladesh and visited our relatives. We ate special food, wore new clothes and my family gave me presents! It was fun.

Your Space

6 **Work in pairs. Talk about what you were doing yesterday.**

What were you doing at ...
3 pm? • 5 pm? • 7 pm? • 9 pm? • 11 pm?

A I was doing my homework at 3 pm. What were you doing?
B I was playing the violin.

Ⓡ   **Past simple and past continuous**

1 **Look at the rules. Then complete the cartoon with these words.**

> had   doing   playing   called

What were you _doing_ yesterday afternoon? I _called_ you but there was no answer.

I was _playing_ rugby. I _had_ an accident.

- Use the past simple to talk about finished events in the past.
  *We **were** in town yesterday evening.*
  *I **watched** a film last night.*

- Many common verbs are irregular in the past.
  *I **saw** my best friend yesterday.*
  *We **went** to a museum on Saturday.*

  Go to page 118 for a list of irregular verbs.

- Use the past continuous to talk about an action in progress in the past.
  *I **was playing** football in the afternoon.*
  *We **were watching** TV all evening.*
  *They **weren't swimming**.*
  ***Was** he **studying** yesterday evening?*

2 🗨 **Work in pairs. Talk about what you did yesterday. Think of at least five things.**

A I played computer games.
B Me too!

3 **Write sentences about what you did yesterday.**

Yesterday I sent five text messages.

4 🗨 **Work in pairs. Look at the picture. Ask and answer questions about the accident.**

1 Ann / ride
2 Lara and Nathan / eat
3 Marissa / paint / a picture
4 Rachel / buy / fruit
5 Vicky / walk / a dog
6 Chris / use his laptop
7 Lara and Nathan / drink / cola
8 Rachel / wait for a bus

A Was Ann riding her bike?
B Yes, she was.

5 ✏ **Write a description of the picture.**

Yesterday there was an accident outside Jake's café. When the accident happened, Ann was riding her bike ...

Yesterday at one o'clock, there was an accident outside Jake's Café. When the accident happened ...

when / while

Get up now!

LONG ACTION   SHORT ACTION

*I **was sleeping when** my dad **came** in the room.*

- Use *when* + past simple to introduce the short action.
  *We were playing chess **when** I got a text message.*
  ***When** I got a text message, we were playing chess.*

- Use *while* or *when* + past continuous to introduce the long action.
  ***While** we were playing chess, I got a text message.*
  ***When** we were playing chess, I got a text message.*

6 (Circle) **the best answer. Sometimes both are possible.**

1 We were eating lunch (when)/ *while* my uncle arrived.

2 I was having a shower *when / while* the phone rang.

3 Were they sitting on the train *when / while* they received the text message?

4 Ethan broke his leg *when / while* he was skateboarding in the park.

5 Where were you going *when / while* I saw you this morning?

6 Enrico met Ruby *when / while* he was living in London.

7 Isabel was listening to Shakira *when / while* she was having her lunch.

8 The teacher wasn't smiling *when / while* we walked into the classroom late.

7 **Complete the text with the correct form of the words in brackets.**

Yesterday afternoon I ¹ was walking (walk) through the park when I ² _____ (see) something very funny. Some boys ³ _____ (play) football. One boy ⁴ _____ (run) with the ball towards the goal when a small dog ⁵ _____ (run) on to the pitch. The boy ⁶ _____ (stop) to look at the dog, and it ⁷ _____ (steal) the ball from him and ⁸ _____ (score) a goal with its nose! The boy ⁹ _____ (be) so shocked, he ¹⁰ _____ (not know) what to do. It ¹¹ _____ (be) hilarious!

8 ☆ **Work in pairs. Talk about your morning. Think of other ideas.**

This morning I ...

| spoke to ... | put ... in my school bag | got up at ... |

| left the house at ... | saw ... | had ... for breakfast |

While I was travelling to school today I ...

| ate an apple | saw my neighbour | talked to ... |

| texted my best friend | finished my homework |

Soundbite

/aʊ/ /əʊ/

A ● 1.02 **Listen and** (circle) **the words you hear.**

1 town   tone
2 now   no
3 loud   load
4 found   phoned

B ● 1.03 **Listen and** (circle) **the /aʊ/ and** underline **the /əʊ/ sounds. Then say the words.**

1 snow   3 house   5 own
2 ground   4 boat   6 down

1B We must finish today

Grammar
must Ⓡ • *have to* Ⓡ • *had to*

Functions
talking about duties and rules

Vocabulary • Websites

1 🔊 **1.04** Complete the sentences with these words. Then listen and check.

> downloaded   uploaded   bookmarked   commented   ~~logged onto~~   posts

Jacob's day on the internet!

1 Jacob _logged onto_ his blogsite.

2 He _____ some photos of his dog, Buddy, for his blog.

3 Then he read the new _____ on the blogsite.

4 He liked a blog, so he _____ on it. He wrote: 'I like your blog. It's interesting.'

5 He _____ some new games from the internet onto his games console.

6 He found some websites about science so he _____ them for later.

Presentation

2 **Warm up** Look at the photos on page 13 and answer the questions.

Who can you see? Where are they? What do you think they are talking about?

3 🔊 **1.05** Listen and read the conversation on page 13. Then answer the questions.

1 Why are they looking after a dog?
2 Why couldn't Nathan sleep?
3 What are Nathan's excuses about the article?
4 When do they have to finish the webzine?
5 When do they go online?
6 What is Holly's idea for the article?

4 Read the *Language focus* sentences. Then answer the questions for each sentence.

sentence	Who is speaking?	Who are they speaking to?	What are they speaking about?
1			
2			
3			
4			
5			

Language focus

- I **had to spend** loads of time with them.
- You **have to write** another article.
- You **don't have to write** a novel.
- You **must make** it interesting.
- You **mustn't stay** out here.

🔘 1.05

A It's Monday morning and Nathan isn't happy.

Holly	Hey, Nathan, are you OK? You look terrible!
Nathan	I'm really tired.
Josh	Why?
Nathan	My cousins were staying with us at the weekend and I had to spend loads of time with them. Then I had to go to my gran's birthday party and I forgot to buy her a present. It was so embarrassing! And we had to look after our neighbours' dog because they're on holiday. It bit a hole in my football, and last night I couldn't sleep because it was making a noise the whole time!
Samira	Well, don't forget the webzine.
Nathan	Why? What do I have to do?
Samira	You have to write another article.
Nathan	I haven't got time! I have to do loads of homework and I'm already in trouble. And I'm not allowed to use my computer after ten o'clock ...
Josh	You don't have to write a novel, Nathan!
Holly	But you must make it interesting.
Samira	And we must finish the webzine today. We go online in the morning and I have to upload it.

B Nathan is worried.

Nathan	But I don't know what to write about!
Holly	OK, OK, I have an idea.
Nathan	What is it?
Holly	Just write about your awful weekend. It's hilarious!
Mr Clark	You mustn't stay out here! It's time for your first lesson!

Your Space Talking about duties and rules

5 Write two answers for you for each question.

1 What do you have to do this week? I have to study for an exam.
2 What did you have to do at the weekend? I had to help my parents.
3 What are your school rules? You mustn't take a mobile to school.

6 Work in pairs. Ask and answer the questions.

A What do you have to do this week?
B I have to go to the library.

Chat zone

It was so embarrassing!
the whole time
I'm not allowed to ...
It's hilarious!

Ⓡ *must / have to*

You can't run faster than a tiger.

I .... have to run faster than the tiger, I just .... run faster than you!

I .... do more exercise.

1 Look at the rules. Then complete the cartoons with these words.

| must   don't   have to |

- You can use *must* or *have to* for rules and obligations.
  I **must** study hard for my exams.
  We **have to** study two languages at my school.

- We usually use *have to*, not *must*, in questions.
  Do we **have to** write the answers down?

- Use *not have to* when an action isn't necessary.
  I **don't have to** tidy my room today.

- The past of *must* and *have to* is *had to*.
  We **had to** tidy our classroom yesterday.

Get it right!

After *must/mustn't* don't use *to*.
You **must** come to my house.
NOT ~~You must to come to my house.~~
You **must** bring paper and a pencil.
NOT ~~You must to bring paper and a pencil.~~

2 Complete the school bus rules with *must* or *mustn't* and the verbs below.

| eat   ~~stand~~   throw   obey |
| keep   chew   stay   shout |

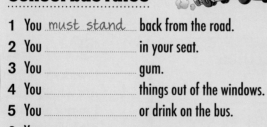

School bus rules

1 You <u>must stand</u> back from the road.
2 You .... in your seat.
3 You .... gum.
4 You .... things out of the windows.
5 You .... or drink on the bus.
6 You ....
7 You .... the bus clean.
8 You .... the driver.

3 🔘 **1.06** Listen to the bus driver and check your answers.

4 🔘 **1.07** Listen to Sophie's interview with Anna and Robbie. Tick (✓) the things they have to do, and cross (✗) the things they don't have to do.

	Anna	Robbie
tidy his/her bedroom		
go to school on Saturday morning		
go to bed before ten o'clock		
text his/her parents if he/she is late		
practise a musical instrument		
study every evening		

5 Write two more questions. Then ask and answer all the questions with your partner.

A Do you have to tidy your bedroom?
B Yes, I do. What about you?

6 Complete the conversation with the correct form of *have to / not have to* and the verbs in brackets. Then act it out.

Leon	Hi there! How was your weekend?
Mia	It was terrible.
Leon	Oh no. Why?
Mia	Well, I ¹ *had to* (✓ study) for an exam all day on Saturday, and then on Sunday I ² _____ (✓ help) my family in the garden.
Leon	³ _____ your brother _____ (help) too?
Mia	No, he didn't. He ⁴ _____ (✓ go) to football practice at school. He ⁵ _____ (✓ train) for a big match.
Leon	Were your parents busy?
Mia	Yeah! They ⁶ _____ (✓ visit) my gran on Saturday. They ⁷ _____ (✓ drive) all the way to Scotland. So how was your weekend?
Leon	Well, I ⁸ _____ (✗ study). And I ⁹ _____ (✗ help) in the house.
Mia	Why not?
Leon	I was at the beach.
Mia	That's so unfair!

7 Write six things you and your family had to do last week.

I had to go to the dentist.
My mum had to take the car to the garage.

8 Work in pairs. Talk about what you had to do last week.

A I had to do lots of science homework.
B Was it difficult?

→ **Language check page 128**

Verbs and prepositions

We use past continuous to talk about a fixed hour in the past.

9 What were these people doing at three o'clock on Saturday? Match the pictures with the sentences.

Isabel was paying for her ticket. ☐
Alice was waiting for the bus. ☐1

Max was talking about his dog. ☐
Alexei was thinking about sport. ☐

Maria was talking to her friend. ☐
Amber was listening to music. ☐

10 Complete the sentences with the correct prepositions.

1 What time did you talk _to_ Liam?
2 My gran always talks _____ the past.
3 Do you enjoy listening _____ music?
4 Please pay _____ your drinks before leaving the café area.
5 We waited _____ you until 7 pm.
6 I don't like thinking _____ sad things.

1C Skills

Reading and speaking

1 **Warm up** Look at the heading and the photos. What do you think the article is about?

2 **Read the article. Then match the photos with the places.**

Tokyo ☐   New York ☐   Sydney ☐   Rio de Janeiro ☐ a   London ☐

3 **Read the article again and make notes about these places.**

> ~~Scotland~~   Kiritimati   New York   Sydney   Rio de Janeiro   London   Tokyo

Scotland: New Year called Hogmanay, four or five day celebrations, traditional music

4 **Work in pairs. Discuss what you and your family do at New Year.**

Do you eat special food? Do you have any special traditions? Do you go outside?

Listening

5 ⊙ **1.09** **Listen and put the New Year's resolutions in order.**

My resolutions

Join a gym	☐
Eat less chocolate	☐
Learn the guitar	☐
Be more polite to my mum	☐
Do more homework	☐
Save some money	1
Go to bed earlier	☐

Writing

6 **Write three New Year's resolutions. Choose from these categories.**

(Health and fitness)   (Hobbies and interests)   (Friends and family)

(Studies)   (Money)   (Lifestyle)

I'm not going to eat any junk food this year.

7 **Work in groups. Tell each other your New Year's resolutions.**

A What are your New Year's resolutions?
B Well, I'm going to save lots of money for my holidays.

Study skills

Chatting
In a conversation, ask questions to get more information. Show interest in the answers. You can say *I see. OK. Right.* or *That's interesting.*

HAPPY NEW YEAR!

New Year's Eve is probably the oldest celebration in the world – it started in Babylonia 4,000 years ago. Most people celebrate it on 31st December.

New Year is a time for making resolutions but it is also about parties, fun and fireworks! There is also special food – in the USA people eat black–eyed peas, and in Europe they make cakes and sweets. In some English–speaking countries people wear paper hats, join hands and sing 'Auld Lang Syne' at midnight. Scotland is famous for its Hogmanay (New Year) celebrations which last four or five days and have traditional Scottish music!

Countries around the world have fireworks and street parties at New Year. Each year, the first place to experience the New Year is Kiritimati (Christmas Island) in the Pacific Ocean. After that, Auckland, New Zealand, is the first large city to celebrate and Alaska is one of the last places. On 31st December it is summer in Australasia. In Europe it is winter, but people still gather outside to celebrate!

2010 was a special New Year because it was the end of the first decade of the 21st century. In New York, hundreds of thousands of people watched a giant crystal ball come down into Times Square. Millions of pieces of confetti floated down with 10,000 handwritten New Year wishes. In Sydney, 1.5 million people watched fireworks over the Opera House, and in Rio de Janeiro about 2 million people gathered on Copacabana beach. In London, 200,000 people listened to Big Ben and watched fireworks over the river Thames. In Tokyo, temple bells rang out at midnight and illuminated balloons floated in the sky.

The New Year is a new beginning and an opportunity to start again, so on 31st December remember to make your New Year's resolutions!

Grammar
will for prediction Ⓡ • *definitely /
probably* • *might / might not* Ⓡ
Functions
talking about the future

Vocabulary • Education

1 Think of a typical day at school. Tick (✓) the things you or your teachers use.

text books ☐   interactive white board ☐   pens and pencils ☐   DVDs ☐   CDs ☐

headphones ☐   notebooks ☐   white board ☐   computers ☐   desks ☐

2 Work in pairs. Discuss the things you and your teachers do on a typical day at school.

A I always sit at the same desk.
B We often listen to CDs in our language lessons.

Presentation

3 **Warm up** Read the introduction to the article on page 19. How do you think school will be different in 2030?

I think students will study new subjects.

4 🔘 **1.12** Listen and read the article. Did you see any of your ideas?

5 Read the article and answer the questions.

1 Why won't students carry bags full of books?
2 How will students study science?
3 What will students study with wireless headphones?
4 What will students see on a big screen?
5 What other things will students study?
6 What will eco schools be like?

6 Read *Language focus*. Then underline more predictions with *definitely, probably, might, might not* and *won't* in the article on page 19.

Language focus

• School buildings **will definitely be** a lot nicer.
• Schools **will probably be** like theme parks.
• Lunches **might be** different.
• The teachers **won't be** in the classrooms.

7 Complete the predictions with *will definitely, will probably, won't* or *might*. Then compare your ideas.

1 Students .... have lessons in schools in the year 2030.
2 There .... be human teachers.
3 Students .... do all their work on computers.
4 Exams .... be easier in the future.
5 Students .... use paper and pens.
6 There .... be lots of trips to museums and exhibitions.

FUTURE SCHOOL 🔘 1.12

What will school be like in the year 2030? How will things change? What will stay the same? Well, we decided to ask the experts for their ideas. That's right. Students just like you ... and some teachers. And this is what they said.

"Students will definitely have e-books. They'll carry one e-book reader and that will be all they need for every subject. They won't have bags full of lots of different coursebooks. It will be great!" *LOLA, STUDENT*

"I think schools will probably be fun places, like theme parks. There won't be any desks! And students will learn through games and by doing things. Maybe they'll study science by building a car or a fridge." *JACOB, STUDENT*

"All students will wear special wireless headphones in language lessons. They'll hear the new language in one ear and a translation in the other ear. It will be really cool!" *HANNAH, STUDENT*

"I think there might not be any teachers – at least, the real teachers won't be in the classrooms. There might be robot teachers in the schools. Students will see their human teachers on their computers. And that will be terrible!" *ISOBEL, TEACHER*

"Students will probably wear virtual reality helmets. Their lessons will be like computer games. When they study the Ancient Romans, they'll 'see' them in virtual reality. The students will think they are in Ancient Rome!" *LOUIS, STUDENT*

"I think students will definitely interact with other schools around the world. There will be a big screen at the front of each classroom. And the class will see students in another classroom in a different country!" *SOPHIE, STUDENT*

"Lunches might be different. The school will have medical and dietary information about all the students. So every individual student will get exactly the food he needs." *MICHAEL, TEACHER*

"Students won't study only subjects like Maths and History. They will definitely learn about being a good citizen. They'll help older people and do work in the community." *TOMASZ, STUDENT*

"School buildings will definitely be a lot nicer. There will be eco schools with lovely gardens and there will be plants in every classroom. And all the energy will come from the sun." *MUHAMMED, STUDENT*

Your Space   Talking about the future

8 Think about next year. Tick (✓) the things you will do and cross (✗) the things you won't do. How certain are you?

learn to play a musical instrument ☐   change my school ☐
go on a school trip ☐   read a book in English ☐   act in a play ☐
pass all my exams ☐   study a new language ☐

9 Work in groups. Talk about your ideas.

A I might act in a play.
B Really? I won't act in a play.
C I'll probably read a book in English.

will / won't • definitely / probably

Oh dear. What **will** we **eat** tomorrow?

I think we**'ll probably eat** fish.

We **definitely won't have** steak.

- Use *will* to make predictions about the future.
  *People **will** use electric cars in 2020.*

- Weather forecasters often use *will*.
  *It **will** be cloudy this afternoon.*

- We often use *think/definitely/probably* to make predictions.
  *I **think** I'll go to university.* (not sure)
  *He'll **definitely** come to the party.* (sure)
  *It **will probably** snow tomorrow.* (not really sure)

1 ⊙ **1.13** Listen and ⟨circle⟩ the correct weather for each city. Then listen again and write the temperatures.

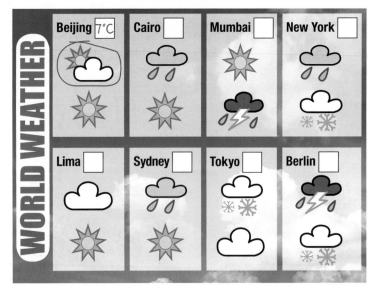

WORLD WEATHER

| Beijing 7°C | Cairo ☐ | Mumbai ☐ | New York ☐ |
| Lima ☐ | Sydney ☐ | Tokyo ☐ | Berlin ☐ |

2 Look at the weather chart again and complete the sentences with *will* or *won't*.

1 It ......*will*...... be cloudy with some sun in Beijing.
2 It .... rain in Cairo.
3 There .... be storms in Mumbai but it .... be hot.
4 It .... snow in New York.
5 It .... be cloudy in Lima.
6 It .... rain in Sydney.
7 It .... be quite cold in Tokyo.
8 It .... be hot in Berlin.

3 🗫 Work in pairs. Talk about the weather.

this evening ▸ tomorrow ▸ at the weekend ▸ next month

A What will the weather be like tomorrow?
B I think it will rain. It won't be cold.
A It will probably be hot.

4 🗫 Work in groups. Make predictions for next year. Use your own ideas or the ideas below.

get a new pet
go on holiday
move home
go to a new school
get better at English
visit another country
study more
watch less TV
make new friends
learn a musical instrument

A I will definitely get a new pet.
B We'll go on holiday to Canada.
C We won't move home.

Get it right!

Use *will/won't* when you are sure and *might/might not* when you are not sure.
I **will** go to the park with you. (sure)
I **won't** see you tomorrow. (sure)
I **might** go to the disco. (not sure)
I **might not** buy that DVD. (not sure)

5 Write sentences with *will/won't, might / might not.*

1 the film / be great (✓ sure)
   The film will be great.
2 we / go the theme park on Saturday
   (✗ not sure)
   We might not go to the theme park on Saturday.
3 Nathan / get into trouble with his parents
   (✓ not sure)
4 The weather / be nice tomorrow (✗ sure)
5 Freya / arrive late at the party (✓ sure)
6 We / go on holiday this year (✗ not sure)
7 Our teacher / give us a lot of homework
   (✗ sure)
8 I / get a lot of birthday cards this year
   (✓ not sure)
9 Rosa and Alessa / go to Canada next year
   (✗ not sure)
10 My sister / learn to drive when she's
    seventeen (✓ sure)

Soundbite

syllables

A ◉ 1.14 Listen and count the syllables. Are there two, three or four?

probably [3]   information [ ]
maybe [ ]   important [ ]
interests [ ]   fortunately [ ]
education [ ]   decisions [ ]
definitely [ ]   environment [ ]
science [ ]   ecology [ ]

B ◉ 1.14 Listen again and repeat.

6 Work in groups. Talk about what you will do next week.
A I'll definitely watch a DVD.
B Which film?
A *Tintin.* I really like it. What about you?
C I might download some music.

We're visiting an eco house

Grammar
will for offers, promises and decisions • present continuous for future and *going to* Ⓡ

Functions
talking about plans

Vocabulary • Green lifestyle

1　🔘 **1.15** **Match the words with the items in the picture. Then listen and repeat.**

wind turbine [4]　solar panels [ ]　energy-saving light bulb [ ]　rainwater tank [ ]
compost bin [ ]　recycling bins [ ]　green roof [ ]　vegetable garden [ ]　tree house [ ]

2　**Work in pairs. Ask and answer questions. How eco-friendly are you?**

Do you ...?

recycle your rubbish • turn off the lights when you leave a room • use energy-saving light bulbs
• walk or cycle to school • turn off the taps in the bathroom • buy recycled paper and notebooks

Presentation

3　**Warm up** **Look at the photo and article on page 23 and answer the questions.**

What do you think Holly's problem is?　What are Holly and Nathan going to do?

4　🔘 **1.16** **Listen and read the dialogue and article. Are the sentences true (*T*) or false (*F*)?**

1　Holly and Nathan are going to visit a special kind of house.
2　Holly can't find any memory cards for her camcorder.
3　Nathan is going to help Holly.
4　Isabelle's house has got solar panels and wind turbines.
5　A computer helps her family save energy.
6　Isabelle is planning to have a tree house.

Language focus

- What **are** we **doing** this afternoon?
- You**'re interviewing** a girl called Isabelle.
- We**'re going to have** wind turbines.

5　**Read *Language focus*. Underline more examples of the present continuous for future and circle examples of *going to* in the article on page 23.**

6　**Look at the diary and write about the Web Crew's plans.**

Monday 4.00 pm	Nathan interview school football team	
Tuesday 7.00 pm	Holly film firework display	
Wednesday 3.00 pm	Josh design new web page	
Thursday 2.00 pm	Samira and Nathan interview at the animal refuge	
Friday 3.00 pm	Samira upload films	

1 On Monday at 4.00 pm Nathan is interviewing the school football team.

1.16

A   Holly and Nathan are checking their plans.

Holly   Hi Nathan.

Nathan Hi there. Holly, what are we doing this afternoon?

Holly   Well, we're leaving at two o'clock and we're visiting an eco house. You're interviewing a girl called Isabelle. And she's got lots of ideas!

Nathan Cool. And don't worry. I'll write my article tomorrow. That's a promise!

Holly   Great ... Oh no, what a pain! My memory card's full. I'll go to the shops and buy a new one.

Nathan That isn't very eco! Why don't you copy your films onto your computer?

Holly   I know, I know, but I'm always so busy and there isn't time ...

Nathan It's OK, I'll get a memory card for you.

Holly   Really? Are you sure?

Nathan No worries. See you later.

webzine

B

The WEB CREW visit an eco house

This week we meet ISABELLE COX

What is the point of an eco house, Isabelle?
Well, I want to help the environment, and my parents want to save money!

So what's different about your house?
Well, we produce a lot of our own energy and we collect and recycle all our rain water in big tanks. And we have a brilliant computer! It turns off the lights and the TV when we leave a room. And it controls the temperature.

What are those things on your roof?
They're solar panels. We get our energy from the sun. Next year we're going to put wind turbines in the garden.

Are you planning to make any other changes?
My dad is going to build me a tree house this summer! I love the idea of reading a book in a tree! We grow our own vegetables already, but we're going to have compost bins with worms in them.

Yuk!
Come on, Nathan, with global warming, we all have to change the way we live.

Your Space   Talking about plans

7   Work in pairs. Ask and answer questions about your plans. Invent times.

this evening • tomorrow • Sunday

A What are you doing at seven o'clock this evening?
B I'm having dinner.

Chat zone

What a pain!
Really?
No worries.

will for offers, promises and decisions

1 🔘 **1.17** **Match the conversations with the pictures. Then complete the conversations with the verbs. Listen and check.**

1 ☐   2 ☐

3 ☐   4 ☐

5 ☐   6 ☐

stay	open	carry	take	borrow	make

a Eva   You haven't taken the dogs for a walk.

  Albert   Don't worry. I'll _____ them for a walk soon.

b King   What do you want to do today?

  Queen   I think I'll _____ a new museum.

c Dan   I'm not very happy about this.

  George   Sorry! I won't _____ your computer again.

d Thief   This picture is really heavy.

  Tom   I'll _____ it for you.

e Mum   What's wrong?

  Dad   I don't feel well. I think I'll _____ at home today.

f Man   I feel very cold.

  Woman   I'll _____ a fire, darling.

2 **Look at the conversations in Exercise 1 again. Are they decisions (*D*), offers (*O*) or promises (*P*)?**

1 _____   3 _____   5 _____

2 _____   4 _____   6 _____

3 **Read the situations and complete the speech bubbles.**

1 Liam wants to talk to you. Promise to call him.

> *I'll call soon.*

2 Your friend, Mike, is going away for the weekend. Promise to look after his dog.

3 A friend is having problems with his computer. Offer to help.

4 There are a lot of dishes to wash. Offer to do it.

5 Your friend, Jess, is coming to visit you. Offer to meet her at the station.

6 Your sister is bored. Promise to play tennis with her later.

4 🗨 **Work in pairs. Act out the conversations in Exercise 3.**

Present continuous and *going to* ®

5 **Match the sentences with the descriptions.**

a talking about fixed arrangements with people

b talking about future plans and intentions

1 I'm going to the gym tomorrow afternoon. ☐

2 I'm playing football with Millie at five o'clock tomorrow. ☐

3 I'm meeting Sam and Ella tonight. ☐

4 I'm going to be a vet when I grow up. ☐

6 ✎ **Work in pairs. Read the instructions.**

- Decide if you are A or B.
- Read the instructions and decide what you are going to say.
- Have the conversation. Then swap roles.

A What are you doing at the weekend?
B I'm going away.
A Where are you going?
B I'm going to Paris in France.

Ask what your partner is doing at the weekend. → Say you are going away.

Ask where your partner is going. → Say where you are going. Choose an interesting place!

Ask who he/she is going with. → Say who you are going with.

Ask how he/she is travelling. → Say how you are travelling.

Ask what time he/she is leaving. → Say when you are leaving.

Tell your partner to have a great weekend!

7 ✎ **Write about your plans for next weekend. Use the present continuous for arrangements and *going to* for intentions.**

Next weekend my uncle and my cousins are coming to our house. We're going to have a picnic and ...

➡ **Language check page 128**

Collocations

Some words go together in pairs or groups. You can often predict what words will come next. This helps you understand more easily.

8 **Complete the phrases with the words in the box.**

a new stadium money a surprise a talk a new song a computer ~~a traditional costume~~ a torch

1 wear *a traditional costume*

2 carry ....

3 get ....

4 save ....

5 build ....

6 use ....

7 learn ....

8 give ....

9 **Use verbs 1–8 in Exercise 8 to make more collocations with the words below.**

a bag   a present   a new language

a paper hat   a reason   a tree house

the internet

get a present

Reading

1 Read the article. Match the headings with the paragraphs.

1 **A new look** 2 **A better future** 3 **Pick up a car!** 4 **Changing energy** 5 **Extreme weather**

CiTY LiFe – 50 Years From today

by Dr Evan Wilde

☐ Climate change is affecting the way we live now, but how will it change our lives in the future? And how will we adapt? I believe in 50 years' time, our cities will be better places to live in.

☐ We will stop using oil and coal. These fossil fuels cause pollution and global warming. Instead, we will use solar energy, wind and water power. However, I believe the answer to our energy needs will be bio fuels such as corn. Bio fuels have many advantages. They are renewable (we can grow them again and again), clean, and take carbon dioxide out of the air. This is important because CO_2 causes global warming!

☐ Global warming will make temperatures go up and so there will be more extreme weather such as hurricanes and floods. Sea levels will get higher. Cities near the sea, such as London and Rio de Janeiro, will need to build very high sea walls to stop floods. Also, there won't be enough water for all our needs. But we will purify sea water so we can drink it. And we will build cleaner, energy-saving homes.

☐ People travel too much – and travelling uses energy and causes pollution. So in the future, people will share cars. How will it work? Well, people will go to a car park, pick up a car, drive it across the city, then leave it in a car park near their destination. When they drive home, they will use a different car. This saves energy. Cars, buses and lorries will use electricity so they will be cleaner, quieter and safer.

☐ I think cities will look different too. In every neighbourhood, homes, shops, restaurants, schools and businesses will be close together. So it will be easy to get to the office or the factory. And don't forget, we will all have computers. Lots of people will work, study and shop at home. When they travel, they will walk or cycle. That's cheap – and good for you, too!

I believe we will be healthier and happier in 50 years' time. Am I crazy? I don't think so. Am I an optimist? Yes, I am! But what do you think?

2 Read the article again and give reasons for these opinions.

1 Bio fuels are better than fossil fuels.
   Bio fuels are renewable and clean. They take CO_2 out of the air.
2 There will be more extreme weather.
3 Cars will be cleaner and quieter.
4 People will travel less.
5 People will be healthier.

3 Match the words with the definitions.

1 pollution   a increase in world temperatures caused by pollution
2 hurricane   b a large amount of water that suddenly covers land
3 global warming   c a powerful storm with very strong winds
4 to purify   d to remove bad substances or chemicals
5 flood   e damage to water, land or air caused by chemicals and waste

Study skills

Guessing meaning
You don't always need a dictionary. You can guess. For example, 'We will **purify** sea water so we can drink it'. What does *purify* mean?

Listening and speaking

4 🔘 **1.19** Listen to students talking about life in the future. (Circle) the optimistic students and underline the pessimistic students.

Joel Katie Charlie Matilda Rosie Elliott

5 🔘 **1.19** Listen again and match the opinions with the students. Write *J* (Joel), *K* (Katie), *C* (Charlie), *M* (Matilda), *R* (Rosie), or *E* (Elliott).

There won't be enough water and countries will fight to get it. ☐

People will be really unhealthy. ☐

Robots will work as shop assistants. ☐

Kids will definitely go to better schools. ☐

Air pollution will get a lot worse. ☐

People will cycle a lot more. ☐

6 Work in groups. Do you agree with the students' opinions? Discuss your own ideas.

A I think robots won't work as shop assistants.
B I don't agree. I think robots will do lots of different jobs.
C I think …

Writing

7 Write your opinions about Dr Evan Wilde's article. Think about:

• Are you optimistic or pessimistic about life in the future?
• How do you think life will change? Give reasons.

Grammar
present perfect ®
ever / never

Functions
talking about experiences

Vocabulary • Physical activities

1 ○ **1.22** **Match the activities with the pictures. Then listen and check.**

go surfing 3   go go-karting 7   do rock climbing 10   do trampolining 8

go ice-skating 9   go skiing 1   go canoeing 2   go scuba diving 5

go skateboarding 4   go mountain biking 6

2 **Work in pairs. Look at the activities in Exercise 1 and discuss these questions.**

Which ones do you do with other people?   Which ones make you the fittest?

Which ones are the most difficult?   Which ones are the most fun?

Presentation

3 **Warm up** **Work in pairs. Ask and answer the questions in the webzine introduction on page 29.**

4 ○ **1.23** **Listen and read the conversation. Then answer the questions. Write *R* (Reuben),
B (Brooke) or *F* (Finlay).**

Who …

1 has dived from a board?   B
2 has slept under the stars?
3 hasn't climbed a tree?

4 has done rock climbing?
5 has been surfing?
6 has raised money for charity?

5 **Read *Language focus*. Then complete the interview with these words.**

| played   been   haven't (x2)   slept   have (x3)   ~~done~~ |

Samira	Have you ever ¹ _done_ trampolining?
Martha	Yes, I ² _have_ . I love it!
Samira	Have you ever ³ _played_ canoeing?
Martha	No, I ⁴ _haven't_ . I don't like water!
Samira	⁵ _have_ you ever played baseball?
Martha	No, I ⁶ _haven't_ . But I've ⁷ _____ basketball.
Samira	Have you ever ⁸ _slept_ in a tent?
Martha	Yes, I ⁹ _have_ .

Language focus

- I**'ve dived** from a board.
- I **haven't climbed** a tree.
- He**'s helped** old people.
- **Have** you **ever swum** in a lake?
- **Have** you **ever been** skiing?
- **Yes, I have. / No, I haven't.**

A
Are you adventurous?

Do you like a challenge?

Do you enjoy learning new skills or taking risks?

Do you like helping people?

Well, let's see what your classmates have done!

Nathan didn't ask the questions this week. He's at home in bed – with flu! So Samira has done the interviews for him!

B **Samira is asking the questions.**

Samira   Hi Reuben.
Reuben   Hi there.
Samira   Reuben, do you like a challenge?
Reuben   Er … yes, I think so. I mean, I love trying new things.
Samira   So what sort of things have you done?
Reuben   I've done some extreme sports. You know, I've done rock climbing, and I've been mountain biking. Oh, and I've slept under the stars!
Samira   How romantic! Where?
Reuben   In my garden!
Samira   Very funny. OK, Brooke. What about you? Do you like a challenge?
Brooke   Yes, I do. I've dived from a board. I've been surfing, too. I love all water sports.

Samira   Have you ever swum in a lake?
Brooke   Yes, I have. Oh, and I've been scuba diving! That's the most exciting activity ever!
Samira   Wow. All right, let's talk to your brother, Finlay. Have you ever been skiing? Or rock climbing?
Finlay   No, I haven't. I haven't climbed a tree. And I've never flown in a plane. Believe it or not, I can't stand heights! It's funny, my sister has done lots of amazing things – but I've never wanted to do them.
Brooke   Yes, but Finlay has raised money for charity. And he's helped old people in the neighbourhood. So he likes a challenge, too. We're very different, that's all. And that's cool.

Your Space   Talking about experiences

6   **Work in pairs. Ask and answer questions about these experiences.**
- been mountain biking? • dived from a board? • slept in a tent?
- been on a rollercoaster? • done trampolining? • swum in a lake?
- done rock climbing? • been surfing? • been canoeing or kayaking?
- been skiing? • climbed a tree? • been sailing?

A Have you ever been mountain biking?
B Yes, I have. / No, I haven't.

Chat zone
Very funny.
Believe it or not
I can't stand …
That's all.

ℝ **Present perfect**

- Use the present perfect to talk generally about your experiences up to now.

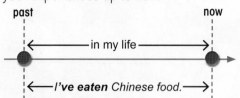

- Don't use the present perfect to talk about an exact moment in the past. Use the past simple. *Last year I* **went** *to India.*

- Use the present perfect when there is a result in the present.

How many films **have** you **been** in?

I've acted in more than fifty films. But no one **has seen** my face!

She **has eaten** all the biscuits.

I**'ve studied** a lot this term.

1 📖 **Do the quiz. What is your score?**

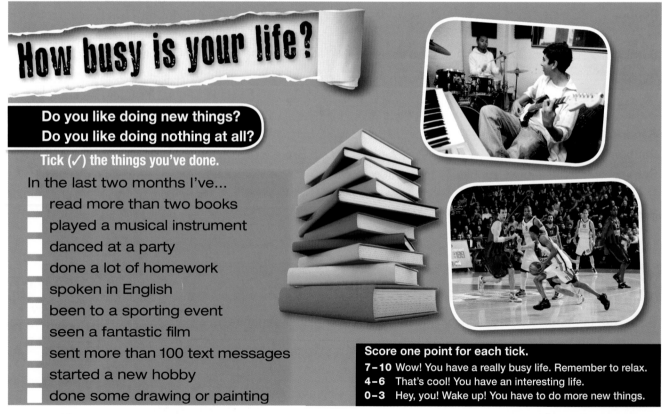

How busy is your life?

Do you like doing new things?
Do you like doing nothing at all?

Tick (✓) the things you've done.

In the last two months I've...

- ☐ read more than two books
- ☐ played a musical instrument
- ☐ danced at a party
- ☐ done a lot of homework
- ☐ spoken in English
- ☐ been to a sporting event
- ☐ seen a fantastic film
- ☐ sent more than 100 text messages
- ☐ started a new hobby
- ☐ done some drawing or painting

Score one point for each tick.

7–10 Wow! You have a really busy life. Remember to relax.
4–6 That's cool! You have an interesting life.
0–3 Hey, you! Wake up! You have to do more new things.

2 🗨 **Work in pairs. Compare your answers.**
A I've read more than two books.
B I haven't read any books!

3 🗨 **Ask round the class. Find a 'yes' answer for each activity and write the name.**
A Have you played a musical instrument in the last two months?
B Yes, I have.

4 Unscramble the verbs and match them with the past participles.

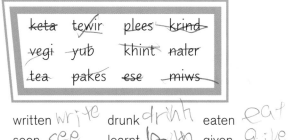

keta   tewir   plees   krind
vegi   yub   khint   nater
tea   pakes   ese   miws

written *write*   drunk *drink*   eaten *eat*
seen *see*   learnt *learn*   given *give*
swum *swim*   slept *sleep*   thought *think*
taken *take*   bought *buy*   spoken *speak*

Get it right!

Go has two past participles: *been* and *gone*.
Be careful to use the right one.
Use *been* to say that a person has recently come back from a place.
What a lot of bags!
Yes, I**'ve been** to the supermarket.
NOT I've gone to the supermarket.
Use *gone* to say that a person is at a place but they haven't come back.
Where's Mum?
She**'s gone** to her tennis class.
NOT She's been to her tennis class.

5 Circle the correct past participle.

1 Where's Dad? He's *been* / *gone* to work.
2 You look tired. Yes, I've *been* / *gone* for a walk.
3 Can I talk to Sara, please? Sorry, she's *been* / *gone* to school.
4 You've got cold hands. Yes, I've *been* / *gone* outside in the snow.
5 Where's the car? Paul has *been* / *gone* to the sports club.
6 Why isn't the teacher here? He's *been* / *gone* to a teachers' meeting.

6 ✎ Write about what you have done / haven't done in the last seven days. Use the verbs below.

send	eat	watch	talk to
visit	play	write	listen to

ever / never

7 🔊 1.24 Listen and tick (✓) the things Jamal has done.

Hi! I'm Jamal.
This is my list of cool things to do before I'm 18.
I've done some of them! What about you?

➤ go to the USA ☐   ➤ go to a car race ☐
➤ climb a mountain ☐   ➤ eat Japanese food ☐
➤ see a play at the theatre ☐   ➤ try surfing ☐
   ➤ ride a horse ☐
➤ play football for my school ☐   ➤ go on a rollercoaster ☐
➤ fly in a plane ☐

8 🗨 Work in pairs and talk about Jamal.

Jamal has been to the USA but he hasn't climbed a mountain.

9 🗨 Ask and answer questions with a partner. Make notes about their answers.
A Have you ever been to the USA?
B Yes, I have.

10 🗨 Tell another student about what your partner has or hasn't done.
Sophie has been to the USA. She hasn't …

Soundbite

/h/

A 🔊 1.25 Listen and repeat the tongue-twisters.

1 Harry hiked in the hills of Hawaii.
2 Holly hired a helicopter for her holidays.
3 Herbert hides his hat when his horse is hungry.
4 Hello, how are you, and who are you here to meet?
5 Hannah's husband hurt his head and had to go to hospital.

B Write your own tongue-twister. Then take turns to read them.

I've been here for hours!

Grammar
present perfect with *for / since* • present perfect and past simple
Functions
talking about duration

Vocabulary • Out and about

1 🔊 **1.26** **Match the words with the pictures. Then listen and check.**

torch 8   matches ☐   sleeping bag ☐   map ☐   compass ☐
first aid kit ☐   insect repellent ☐   sun cream ☐   cooking stove ☐   pillow ☐

Presentation

2 **Warm up** **Read the leaflet on page 33 and answer the questions.**

Which items from Exercise 1 does it mention? Do you think the survival course is different from a normal camping holiday? How?

3 🔊 **1.27** **Listen and read the article on page 33. Then answer the questions.**

1 How long is the survival course?
2 When did Skye last have something to eat?
3 What did she do last night?
4 Why has Archie made two shelters?
5 What two things has Georgia achieved?
6 What was the best thing about her meal?

4 **Read *Language focus*. Then underline more sentences with *for* and *since* and the present perfect in the article on page 33.**

Language focus

• I've been here **since** Saturday.
• I've been here **for** 62 hours!

5 **Complete the sentences with *for* or *since*.**

1 Abi has made three new friends .... Saturday.
2 We've looked for food .... three hours, and we haven't found any!
3 Marek and Ben are still asleep. They have been asleep .... ten hours!
4 I haven't sent any text messages .... last weekend.

The Bushcraft School

We teach you how to live with nature and respect the environment. You will learn essential survival skills – and have great fun, too!

Survival course info

Minimum age: 12 years
Maximum age: 16 years

All you need is a sleeping bag, a first aid kit, sun cream and insect repellent, a torch and a wash kit.

On the five-day junior survival course, you will learn how to:

▷ build a shelter
▷ light a fire (without matches!)
▷ navigate by the sun and the stars
▷ follow animal tracks
▷ collect and purify water
▷ cook the food you find

In the wild...

🔘 1.27

You've watched lots of survival programmes on TV. The presenters have built shelters, they've lit fires, and they've cooked food – and it all looks quite easy. But what is surviving in the wild really like? I've joined three young adventurers on a five-day survival course. It's now Day Three, and things are getting difficult!

"I haven't eaten anything since seven o'clock this morning. I'm feeling very hungry. But I'm also having a fantastic time! I've learned lots of new skills. The best thing I've learned is how to navigate by the stars. Last night we went for a long walk in the dark. I was very happy when we got back to our tent safely!" *Skye*

"I've been here since Saturday. To be precise, I've been here for 62 hours! And it feels like 62 days! I've made two shelters. Why two? Well, the first one I made fell down on Saturday night! It was very windy. I hope my mum isn't reading this, because I haven't washed for two days! It's too cold!" *Archie*

"I've done two amazing things today. I've lit a fire and I've cooked a meal! This morning we looked for wild food, and we found some edible leaves and mushrooms (our course tutor said they were OK to eat!). The meal was horrible, but it was hot, and that was the most important thing!" *Georgia*

Your Space   Talking about duration

6 Complete the sentences for you. Use *for* or *since*.

- I have lived in my home ...
- I have known my best friend ...
- I have been a student at this school ...
- I haven't used my mobile phone ...

7 Work in pairs. Compare your answers.
A How long have you lived in your home?
B For six years.

Present perfect with *for* / *since*

1 **Read the rules. Then complete the sentences with the present perfect of the verbs in the box. Use *for* or *since*.**

| be   not do   live   visit   have   play |

- Use the present perfect to talk about experiences which started in the past and continue up to now.
- Use *for* to speak about a period of time.

two years ago   now
←————— for two years —————→

She **has lived** in London
for two years

- Use *since* to talk about the moment when an activity started.

March 2010   now
←——— since March 2010 ———→

I **have known** my best
friend **since** March 2010

Isobel _has been_ in the school football team _for_ six months.

Luka _has visited_ fifteen countries _since_ January.

Lola and Lily _have sung_ five number one singles _since_ 2009.

Henry _has not done_ any exercise _for_ two years.

Lexi _has talked_ on the phone _for_ two hours.

Tilly and Rhys _have lived_ in Australia _since_ 2007.

2 **Match the time expressions with *for* and *since*.**

| ~~Friday~~   ~~three weeks~~   my birthday
half an hour   six years   last weekend
ten minutes   four o'clock   2012
September   two months |

For	Since
three weeks	Friday

3 ☆ **Work in pairs. Ask and answer the questions. Use *for* and *since*.**

How long ...?

| be in this lesson |
| have your school bag |
| live in your home |
| know your best friend |
| have your shoes |
| know your teacher |
| have a pet |
| be at this school |

A How long have you been in this lesson?
B For about 20 minutes. / Since eleven o'clock.

Present perfect and past simple

- We often start a conversation in the present perfect. This is to talk about past experiences in general.
  I've been to Egypt.

- But we often continue with the past simple. This is to give more information.
  I've been to Egypt. I went last year. I visited the Pyramids and went on a trip down the Nile.

- When we use the past simple, we often use time expressions, e.g. *yesterday, last week, a year ago.*
  I rode on a camel last year.

4 ◉ **1.28** Listen and write Max's answers.

The best ever!

1 the best film / see

....

2 the best food / eat

....

3 the best place / visit

....

4 the most interesting person / meet

....

5 the most exciting thing / do

....

5 🗨 **Work in pairs. Ask and answer the questions from Exercise 4. Give your partner extra information.**

A What's the best film you've ever seen?
B The best film I've ever seen is *War Horse.* I saw it a year ago. It's really exciting.

6 ✏ **Choose two topics from Exercise 4 and write a paragraph about each one.**

The best food I've ever eaten is Mexican. I went to a Mexican restaurant on my birthday last year with my friends. We ate tortillas with chicken and vegetables. There were really delicious sauces with tomato and avocado, too. Some of the food was quite spicy but I liked it a lot.

Use of *have*

Have is a very useful verb. Here are the most common ways to use it.

7 **Complete the sentences.**

possessions

1 I've........ got two sisters. We .... got a big house.

experiences

2 My sister .... visited Moscow.

rules

3 We................ to go to school on Monday.

routines

4 In the morning I .... a shower. We all .... cereal for breakfast. I .... lunch at school. My sister usually .... sandwiches.

activities

5 Last month my sister .... a party for her 18th birthday. She and her friends .... a good time!

⯈ **Language check page 129**

Reading and listening

1   **Warm up** Organise the words and phrases into the word pools. Then look at the factfile below and add other examples.

playing the guitar   ~~lifesaving~~   archery   cookery   helping older people   photography
horse riding   collecting rubbish   rock climbing   baseball   being a DJ for a hospital

physical activities and sports

hobbies and interests

lifesaving
volunteering

TAKE THE CHALLENGE & HAVE FUN!

Have you ever felt bored? Would you like to go on an adventure? Well, the International Award for Young People could be just the thing for you!

FACTFILE
BRONZE AWARD

1 Service *15 hours*
Volunteer and make a difference. You can help children or adults, animals or the environment, a charity or an emergency service.

2 Skills *six months*
Develop personal interests and learn new skills – for example, in theatre or music, gardening, chess, or even in car repairs.

3 Physical recreation
30 hours over 15 weeks
Improve your skills in a sport – for example, a team game, athletics, water sports or martial arts.

4 Adventurous journey *two days*
Find your spirit of adventure. Go with a group on a trip or expedition.

Over 6 million 14 to 25 year-olds in one hundred countries have done some amazing things! They have been on expeditions, sailed boats, ridden camels, performed in the circus, made films, worked with animals and helped in hospitals. They did this on a scheme called 'The International Award for Young People'. It started over 50 years ago when the Duke of Edinburgh created an adventure programme for UK teenagers. Now 14 to 25 year-olds in more than one hundred countries can do the award.

It isn't a race, it's a journey

The Award has three levels – Bronze, Silver and Gold. You have to do activities in four different sections. You help other people, learn a new skill, do a sport and go on an adventure trip. And the programme takes at least six months. Sounds difficult? Don't worry, your trainer meets you, gives advice and follows your progress.

I've made lots of friends and learnt a lot

The Award is all about personal challenge, not competition against other people. You don't have to be talented, but you have to make an effort. Doing the award helps you get fit, develop personal skills, learn new things and take responsibility. It gives you skills for life.

It's such fun!

2 **Read the article. Are the sentences true (*T*) or false (*F*)?**

1 Six million 14 to 25 year-olds have been on expeditions.   F
2 The International Award for Young People started in the UK.
3 The Award has four levels.
4 You can help people, learn a new skill, do a sport or go on an adventurous journey.
5 You can't take longer than six months to do the programme.
6 You get help while you do the Award.

Study skills

True/False questions
Be careful when you answer these questions! They can look true but actually be false. For example, question 1 contains the number 'six million', but that is how many 14 to 25 year-olds have been on the scheme, not how many have been on an expedition.

3 🔘 **1.30** **Listen to the radio programme and complete the table.**

	Esha	Matt	Li
Where from?	Delhi India	Perth	Ontario
Service	teach .... to street children	work with disabled children	collect .... from parks for a charity
Skills	made blogs	learn to be a .... referee	learn to write some
Physical recreation	traditional Indian dances	improve my	learn ....
Adventurous journey	trek in the .... and go river canoeing	trek into the outback and .... in difficult conditions	.... in a nature reserve .... a mountain

Speaking and writing

4 **Work in groups. Imagine you are planning an adventure journey. Use the notes to help you.**

- How do you want to travel? (on foot, by canoe, by bicycle, by boat, on horseback)
- Where will you go? What will you do? Who will you go with?
- What will you take?
- Where will you sleep? (tent, build a shelter, youth hostel)
- Who is going to help you? (parents, teachers, relatives)
- What would you like to learn?
- How will you record your experiences? (blog, film, diary, photos)

5 **Write a paragraph describing your planned expedition.**

I'm going trekking in Nepal with my friends, Cameron and Layla, ...

I haven't bought her a present yet

Vocabulary • Shopping

1 Tick (✓) the things you buy.

magazines ☐　clothes ☐　shoes ☐　make-up, shampoo, hair gel ☐　DVDs ☐
music ☐　jewellery ☐　soft drinks, crisps, sweets, chocolate ☐　computer games ☐

2 Work in pairs. Discuss what you spend your money on.

A I buy lots of clothes and shoes.

B I don't. I spend my money on music and DVDs.

Presentation

3 **Warm up** Look at the photos on page 39 and answer the questions.

Who can you see? What do you think is happening?

4 ⊙ **1.33** Listen and read the conversations on page 39. Then answer the questions.

1　What is happening in half an hour?
2　Is Josh's mum at home?
3　What has Keira done?
4　Why hasn't Josh chosen the music?
5　What has he made on his computer?
6　Why was his text message a mistake?

Language focus

- I've **just** sent her a text.
- I've **already** lit the barbecue.
- I **haven't** done that **yet**.
- Have you tidied up the living room **yet**?

5 Read *Language focus*. Then underline examples of *just* and *already*, and circle examples of *yet* in the conversations.

6 Look at Josh's dad's list and complete the sentences.

1　Dad ___has___ already ___lit___ the barbecue.
2　Keira ___has___ already ___tidyed___ the living room.
3　Keira ___has___ just ___put up___ the decorations.
4　Josh ___hasn't___ _____ the music yet.
5　Dad ___has___ already ___made___ the food.
6　Josh ___hasnt___ ___bought___ his mum's present yet.

light the barbecue ✓
tidy up the living room ✓
put up decorations ✓
choose the music ✗
prepare the food ✓
bought Mum's present ✗

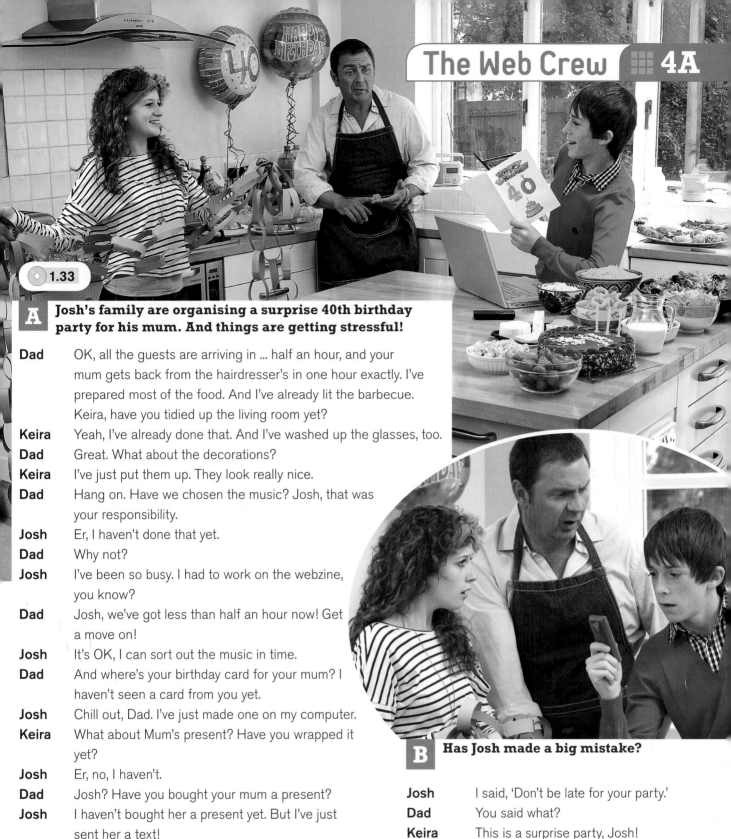

A
Josh's family are organising a surprise 40th birthday party for his mum. And things are getting stressful!

🔘 **1.33**

Dad	OK, all the guests are arriving in … half an hour, and your mum gets back from the hairdresser's in one hour exactly. I've prepared most of the food. And I've already lit the barbecue. Keira, have you tidied up the living room yet?
Keira	Yeah, I've already done that. And I've washed up the glasses, too.
Dad	Great. What about the decorations?
Keira	I've just put them up. They look really nice.
Dad	Hang on. Have we chosen the music? Josh, that was your responsibility.
Josh	Er, I haven't done that yet.
Dad	Why not?
Josh	I've been so busy. I had to work on the webzine, you know?
Dad	Josh, we've got less than half an hour now! Get a move on!
Josh	It's OK, I can sort out the music in time.
Dad	And where's your birthday card for your mum? I haven't seen a card from you yet.
Josh	Chill out, Dad. I've just made one on my computer.
Keira	What about Mum's present? Have you wrapped it yet?
Josh	Er, no, I haven't.
Dad	Josh? Have you bought your mum a present?
Josh	I haven't bought her a present yet. But I've just sent her a text!
Keira	What did you say in your text?

B
Has Josh made a big mistake?

Josh	I said, 'Don't be late for your party.'
Dad	You said what?
Keira	This is a surprise party, Josh!
Josh	Oops!

Your Space Talking about recent events

7 Tick the items from Exercise 1 you have bought this month.

8 Work in pairs. Tell your partner about the things you have/haven't bought this month.

A I've bought some magazines.
B Me too. I've bought a DVD. I bought *The Smurfs* last weekend!

Chat zone
… you know?
Get a move on.
Hang on.

Present perfect with *just*

1 **Match the sentences with the pictures.**

1 The cat has just eaten a fish.

2 Toby has just found the TV remote control.

3 Mia has just scored a goal.

A

B
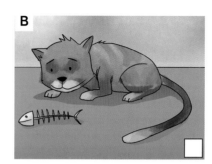

C

2 **Complete the sentences with *just* and the present perfect of the verbs in the box.**

> finish   fall   ~~buy~~   play   arrive

1 She 's just bought a new computer game.

2 Leah's grandparents ....

3 The film ....

4 Andrei .... a football game.

5 Mr Reeves .... off his bike.

3 ✍ **Work in groups. Invent as many explanations as you can for these situations.**

> You're at the top of a mountain.

> You're very tired.   Your mum is surprised.

> Your friend has got muddy shoes.

> Your teacher is annoyed.   You're very happy.

> You and your friend are leaving a building.

You're at the top of a mountain
A I've just climbed up
B I've just arrived in a helicopter

Present perfect with *already / yet*

- Use *not yet* to say a situation is continuing but we expect it to change.

> I **haven't finished** my homework **yet**.

- Use *yet* in questions to ask about a situation we expect to change.

> **Have** you **taken** your vitamin pills **yet**?

- Use *already* to say that an activity happened sooner than we expect.

> I've **already seen** that film.

4 **1.34** Listen to an interview with Billy Dove. Tick (✓) the things he has already done, cross (✗) the things he hasn't done yet.

Teen Spirit

Meet Billy Dove:
The Winner of this
year's Top Talent Show

1 go on a chat show ☐
2 record a hit single ☐
3 travel to the USA ☐
4 buy a big house ☐
5 make a music video ☐
6 meet any famous people ☐
7 do a concert in London ☐

5 ✏ **Write sentences about the things Billy has and hasn't done.**

He's already been on a chat show.

Get it right!

Be careful to use *already* and *yet* in the right places.

I have **already** finished my drink.
NOT ~~I already have finished my drink.~~
Have you cleaned your teeth **yet**?
NOT ~~Have you yet cleaned your teeth?~~

6 🗨 **Work in pairs. Take it in turns to interview another Top Talent Show winner. Talk about the activities in Exercise 4.**

A Hi Corey.
B Hi.
A Have you been on a chat show yet?
B Yes, I have. In fact, I've already been on three chat shows. It was fun.

7 🗨 **Work in pairs. Talk about what you have or haven't done today.**

- have breakfast
- have lunch
- send a text message to a friend
- speak to my best friend
- use a computer

A I haven't sent a text message yet.
B I have. I've already sent texts to 15 friends.
A Amazing!

Soundbite

/θ/ /ð/

A 🔘 **1.35** Listen and (circle) the /θ/ sounds and underline the /ð/ sounds.

1 I bought three new things on Thursday.
2 I think that's a silly idea, Ruth.
3 This is my brother, Theo.
4 Friday the thirteenth is the worst day ever!
5 Thanks for helping with my Maths homework.
6 There are thirty-three students in our class.

B 🔘 **1.35** Listen again and repeat.

4B A typical teen

Grammar
indefinite pronouns
too / too much / too many / (not) enough ®

Functions
giving opinions

Vocabulary • People

1   We often need to talk about people in general. Add these words and expressions to the word maps.

~~teenagers~~   ~~men~~   middle-aged people   boys   young people   kids
old people   students   girls   babies   toddlers   women

children   teenagers   men   **adults**

Presentation

2   **Warm up** Look at the photo on page 43 and try to answer the questions.

What is the relationship between the people? How old are they?

3   🔘 **1.36**   Listen and read the web page. Do the teens think these things are positive (*P*) or negative (*N*)?

having a laugh ⬚P   not enough money ⬚   family tells me off ⬚   freedom ⬚
arguments with parents ⬚   pressure ⬚   chilling out ⬚   nowhere to go ⬚
not paying bills ⬚   being treated like a child ⬚   stress ⬚

4   <u>Underline</u> the opinions in the web page on page 43 and make a note of them.

Tigerboy ...
He likes having a laugh.
He doesn't have enough money.
Everybody tells him off.

5   Work in pairs. Which teenagers do you agree/ disagree with?

A I agree with tigerboy. My parents always tell me off.
B I don't agree with chikita. There are lots of things for teenagers to do in our town.

6   Read *Language focus*. Find and <u>underline</u> other examples in the web page.

Language focus

• **Nothing** is easy.
• **Everybody** tells me off.
• I can't do **anything** right.
• Do **something**!
• There's **nowhere** to go.
• Not **everything** is bad.

Being a teen

Do you feel moody, sleep in late, forget things, argue with your parents? Then you're a typical teen. It's a time of change – you aren't a kid any more. You're growing up. But surely adults should understand? After all, they were teens once! Tell us the best and worst things about being a teen. ● 1.36

 tigerboy
I like having a laugh with my friends. But I don't have enough money to buy anything. And everybody tells me off. My mum, my dad, even my dog when I forget to take him for a walk ☹. It's not fair. I can't do anything right.

 cherri
Being a teen is great fun, but it's stressful, too. Nothing is easy. I have arguments with my parents about nothing. There's too much pressure, too. Will I pass my exams? Will I get a job? Will the world be safe?

 dragonguy
When I'm listening to music, texting my friends, playing computer games, my parents ask, 'What are you doing?' And I say, 'Nothing.' And they say, 'Do something!' But there's nothing wrong with chilling out!

 chikita
My parents are cool – they've given me more freedom, but there isn't enough for teenagers to do in my town and there's nowhere to go. The best thing? I don't have anything serious to worry about. We don't have to earn money, buy food or pay bills.

 greenplanet
I want to be independent, but my parents treat me like a child. There are too many rules. Nobody at home understands me. But not everything is bad! My friends are cool. We hang out and have fun at the weekend.

Your Space　Giving opinions

7　Complete the sentences with your opinions.

- The best thing about being a teen is ....
- The worst thing about being a teen is ....
- The best thing about being an adult is ....
- The worst thing about being an adult is ....

8　Work in groups. Compare your answers.

Chat zone

having a laugh
tells me off
there's nothing
　wrong with …

Indefinite pronouns

1 **Look at the table and complete the cartoons with an appropriate indefinite pronoun.**

somewhere anything everything anywhere

Where does a gorilla sit?
.... it wants!

What time is it if you find an elephant in your bed? Time to sleep .... else!

	people	things	places
some	somebody someone	something	somewhere
any	anybody anyone	anything	anywhere
every	everybody everyone	everything	everywhere
no	nobody no one	nothing	nowhere

We usually use *anybody* etc. in questions. But you can use *something* in questions to offer or request things.
*Is **anybody** going to the party?*
*Would you like **something** to drink?*

What do you get if you cross a parrot with an elephant? An animal that tells you .... it remembers.

Why did Robin Hood only rob the rich?
Because the poor didn't have .... to steal!

2 **Look at the picture. Are the sentences true (*T*) or false (*F*)?**

1 Everybody is wearing trainers. F
2 There isn't anything to eat.
3 Nobody is eating.
4 Somebody is wearing a hat.
5 There is nowhere to put the tray of pizzas.
6 There is nothing to drink.
7 Everybody is dancing.
8 Somebody is watching TV.
9 There is a dog somewhere in the room.
10 Nobody is texting.

3 ✏ **Complete the sentences for you.**

| Something I like wearing is … |

| Somewhere I like hanging out is … |

| Somewhere beautiful in my country is … |

| Somebody I admire is … |

4 🗫 **Work in pairs. Talk about your answers.**

A Something I like wearing is this watch.
B Why do you like wearing it?
A It was a birthday present from my parents, and I think it's cool.

Ⓡ *too / too much / too many / (not) enough*

5 **Complete the comments page with** *too*, *too much*, *too many*, **or** *(not) enough*.

> Have you got anything to complain about? Tell us now.

 There isn't ¹ __enough__ for teenagers to do in my town. *Panos*

 There's ² too much homework to do in my year. *Maxine*

 I've never got ³ enough money. *Luka*

 The cafés in my town are ⁴ too expensive. *Lilly*

 I haven't got ⁵ enough free time. *Matt*

 My parents are ⁶ too strict. *Amy*

 We have to study ⁷ too many subjects. *Ellis*

6 🗫 **Work in groups. What do you want to complain about? Talk about ideas from Exercise 5. Or think of other ideas.**

A There's too much traffic on the streets.
B I agree. It's dangerous on my bike.

➤ **Language check page 129**

Multi-word verbs

Multi-word verbs combine prepositions with common verbs. These are all verb + *up*:
wake up, get up, stand up, tidy up, hurry up

Here are some more:

put up
She's put up a poster.

grow up
My little brother has really grown up!

give up
We have given up chocolate for charity.

dress up
We've dressed up for the parade.

7 **Work in pairs. Take turns to ask and answer the questions.**

1 What posters have you put up in your bedroom?
2 How often do you tidy up your bedroom?
3 Have you ever given something up?
4 Who washes up in your family?
5 What do you want to do when you grow up?
6 Have you ever dressed up in a fancy-dress costume?

Reading

1 Match the words with the definitions.

1	advert		**a**	to increase to cover a larger area
2	display		**b**	a collection of objects in a shop window for people to look at
3	resources		**c**	materials that we use to make things
4	to spread		**d**	to stop yourself from doing something that you want to do
5	to resist		**e**	picture, film, song or word that helps sell a product

Have you ever bought something that you didn't really need? It looked nice in the shop. There was an advert. You wanted it. All your friends had one. There are lots of excuses!

We throw away millions of mobile phones and computers every year. They aren't broken, we just want the latest model. But buying too much is bad for the environment because it creates pollution and uses up the world's resources. It is also expensive. It is better to buy less, and recycle or repair the things that we already have.

Could you survive a whole day without buying anything? Well, on the last Friday in November people around the world celebrate 'International Buy Nothing Day'. They buy absolutely nothing for 24 hours!

A Canadian artist called Ted Dave created the day in 1992. And the idea has spread around the world since then, and gets bigger every year. Nowadays, people in over 60 countries hold 'BND' protests including the UK, Austria, Germany, New Zealand and Japan.

You can celebrate Buy Nothing Day in different ways. You can organise fun activities such as silly protests in shopping centres with balloons, dancing, singing and music. Some protesters dress up in zombie costumes, or set up a market stall where they swap the things they don't want.

Not everyone likes Buy Nothing Day. Some TV channels refuse to advertise it and some people say that the protesters just buy more things the next day. Other people say that factories and shops give people jobs, or that BND is just a protest for people with too much money, because poor people only buy a few things. What do you think? Does Buy Nothing Day encourage us to produce less waste and think about what we buy?

2 Read the article on page 46 and answer the questions. Then compare your answers with a partner.

1 What is wrong with buying things you don't need?
2 When is 'Buy Nothing Day'?
3 Who started it and when did they start it?
4 What do people do on BND?
5 What are some of the criticisms of BND?
6 What do you think about BND?

Study skills

***wh-* questions**
Questions starting *When ...? Who ...? What ...? Where ...?* ask for specific information. Read the article carefully and <u>underline</u> the information before you write your answer.

Listening and speaking

3 ◉ **1.38** Read the questionnaire. Copy the questions into your exercise book. Then listen to the three people and make notes of their answers.

	Person 1	Person 2	Person 3
What have you just bought?			
Do you need it/them?			
How many do you already have?			
How long will you use it/them?			
What will you do when you don't want it/them any more?			
Is it / are they made of recyclable materials?			

Were you born to shop? Or do you think twice before you spend your money?

Think about something you bought last week (e.g. clothes, jewellery, games, gadgets) and answer the questions.

4 Work in groups. Ask and answer the questions from Exercise 3.

Writing

5 Write two paragraphs: one for and one against Buy Nothing Day.

<u>Useful expressions</u>
I think ...   In my opinion ...   I don't believe ...   I'm not sure ...
because/or/so/too   a good/bad idea

5A If you ...

Vocabulary • Illness and injuries

1 🔘 2.02 **Match the people with the pictures. Then listen and check.**

Kira has got stomach ache.	7
Chloe has broken her arm.	
Ajay has got a cold.	
Lucy has cut her finger.	
Anna has got a sore throat.	
Ivan has got a cough.	
Liam has got a headache.	
Joel has got earache.	
Alina has got toothache.	
Dave feels sick.	
Hugo has hurt his hand.	
Mia has got a temperature.	

2 Work in pairs. Choose five people from Exercise 1. Write what they should/shouldn't do. Use the words in the box to help you.

> go to the doctor's   go to the dentist's   go to the hospital   take a tablet
> lie down   drink lots of water   not eat anything   not go to school

Kira shouldn't eat anything. She should go to the doctor's.

Presentation

3 🔘 2.03 **Read and listen to the webzine on page 49. Match the names (diamondlife, PinkPink, neon) with the advice.**

1 You should still go to school.   neon
2 You shouldn't spend so long texting your friends.
3 You should do some exercise.

4 You should talk to your parents.
5 You should take breaks.
6 You should ignore him.

4 Read *Language focus*. Underline other examples of *if* sentences in the webzine.

Language focus

- If you **break** a leg, you **go** to a hospital.
- If you **want** the answer to a question, **write** to us today.
- If you **talk** to your friends on the phone, you**'ll get** better soon!

2.03

Don't worry, be happy!

If you break a leg, you go to a hospital. If you have a toothache, you go to the dentist. It's obvious. But where do you go if you just want some friendly advice? If you want the answer to a question, write to us today! Get advice from the Web Doctor.

Dear Web Doctor
I'm getting a pain in my right thumb. It really hurts! But I don't do weightlifting or anything like that. I just send hundreds of texts! *diamondlife*

Dear diamondlife
You've got texting thumb! First, you should try to use both thumbs. Secondly, you shouldn't write very long messages. And if you talk to your friends on the phone, you'll get better soon!
The Web Doctor

Dear Web Doctor
I have some important exams next month and I'm really worried. I can't sleep at night and then I feel tired and I can't concentrate. I'm so stressed out. What should I do? *PinkPink*

Dear PinkPink
Nobody likes exams, but we all have to take them! You should plan your work and only revise at fixed times. If you do some exercise, you'll think more clearly. And if you listen to some relaxing music, you'll sleep better.
The Web Doctor

Dear Web Doctor
There's a new boy in my class and he calls me horrible names. I'm feeling down and I don't want to go to school. I haven't talked to anyone about this. *neon*

Dear neon
Firstly – it's not your fault! And please don't stop going to school. I think the new boy is a bully. If you talk to your parents and teachers, they will take action. Remember – if you ignore him, he'll get bored. Maybe then he will leave you alone.
The Web Doctor

Your Space   Giving advice

5 **Work in pairs. Give advice to these people.**

1 **Alexis**   My parents don't let me go out with my friends.
2 **Miguel**   I can't get up in the morning.
3 **Zoe**   My six-year-old sister takes my things and never asks my permission.
4 **Ana**   My best friend and I have had an argument. We aren't talking.
5 **William**   My parents won't let me play computer games.

Useful phrases:
If you …, you will…   Why don't you …?   You should …

Chat zone
I'm so stressed out
I'm feeling down
It's not your fault!

Zero conditional

- Use the zero conditional to talk about results of facts.

  if + present simple + present simple

  If the temperature **goes down** to 0°C, water **freezes**.

- Use the zero conditional for imperatives.

  If you **want** to print a document, **press** 'P'.

1 Match the beginnings of the sentences with the endings.

1 If you heat water to 100°C, [f]
2 If you go out in the sun, [d]
3 If a plane flies faster than sound, [c]
4 If astronauts spend time in the Skylab, [e]
5 If there's no oxygen, [b]
6 If you multiply any number by zero, [a]

a the answer is zero.
b things can't burn.
c there is a loud noise.
d your body produces vitamin D.
e they get taller.
f it boils.

2 💬 Work in pairs. Discuss the questions.

Science Mysteries!
What do you think?

❶ **What do you get if you mix red and blue?**

❷ **If you travel away from the Sun, what is the next planet you get to?**

❸ **On the moon, if you drop a kilo of feathers and a kilo of chocolate, which one lands first?**

❹ **If you don't breathe while you're eating, how does food taste?**

❺ **If you make a noise under water, does it travel slower than through the air?**

A If you mix red and blue, you get black.
B I don't agree. If you mix red and blue, you get purple.

3 Look at the leaflet and match the beginnings of the sentences with the endings.

EARTHQUAKE ALERT
If there is an earthquake …

1 If you are indoors, ☐
2 If you are outdoors, ☐
3 If there is a lift, ☐
4 If you are in a car, ☐
5 If you smell gas after the quake, ☐
6 If it's dark after the quake, ☐
7 If the quake stops, ☐

a leave the building because there might be an explosion.
b don't use it, use the stairs.
c stay where you are because the car protects you.
d stay there and hide under a table.
e don't move for a few minutes because there can be aftershocks.
f don't turn on light switches.
g move away from buildings to an open area.

4 ✏ Write advice for these situations.

1 If you visit my capital city, …
2 If you have an important test tomorrow, …
3 If you want to get fit, …

5 💬 Work in groups. Compare your advice. Decide on the best ideas.

First conditional

If it's sunny tomorrow, we'**ll have** a picnic.

- Use the first conditional to talk about possible future events.
  If + present simple + will
  If you **study** *hard, you* **will pass** *the test.*

6 Write first conditional sentences.

1 If / Julia invite me / I go to her party
   If Julia invites me, I'll go to her party.

2 If / it not rain / we play tennis

3 If / you read this book / you love it

4 If / I save enough money / I buy some new speakers

5 If / you not leave now / you miss the bus

6 If / Jake buy a new mp3 player / he give me his old one

Get it right!

Use *will* in the result, NOT in the condition part.
If I have time, I **will watch** that DVD.
NOT ~~If I will have time, I will watch that DVD.~~

7 Complete the sentences for you.

1 I will feel sad if …

2 If I go away on holiday this summer, …

3 If I stay up very late tonight, …

4 I will feel very happy if …

5 Our teacher won't be happy if …

6 If I don't get up tomorrow morning, …

8 Work in pairs. Compare your sentences.

9 2.04 Match the problems with the advice. Then listen and check.

1 I can't get up in the morning.   c

2 I haven't got enough money.

3 My brother eats all my chocolate.

4 My best friend isn't talking to me.

5 I want to be a vet.

6 I don't understand science.

a Why don't you read some books about animals?

b You should offer him some but tell him it's yours.

c If you go to bed early, you'll have more energy.

d Why don't you save your pocket money?

e If you talk to your friend, you'll find out the problem.

f You should ask your teacher more questions.

10 Write a piece of advice for each problem.

11 Work in groups. Choose a problem from Exercise 9 and ask for advice. Decide on the best advice.

A I can't get up in the morning.
B If you go to bed early, you won't be so tired.
C Why don't you do more exercise?

Soundbite

/w/ /v/

A 2.05 Complete the words with *w* or *v*. Then listen and check.

A ....here ....ill you go if it's nice at the ....eekend?

B ....e'll go for a ....alk along the ri....er. Then ....e'll dri....e to some pretty ....illages.

A ....hat if the ....eather's ....et and ....indy?

B ....e'll ....isit some relati....es who li....e by the sea. Or ....e'll stay at home and ....atch T....!

B Work in pairs. Act out the conversation.

5B People who bully ...

Grammar
relative pronouns

Functions
defining and explaining •
joining information

Vocabulary • Behaviour

1 Work in pairs. Do the expressions describe positive (*P*) or negative (*N*) behaviour?

1 **a** tell lies [N]   **b** tell jokes [P]
2 **a** get on with someone ☐   **b** fight someone ☐
3 **a** laugh at someone ☐   **b** have a laugh together ☐
4 **a** hurt someone ☐   **b** help someone ☐
5 **a** look after things ☐   **b** damage things ☐
6 **a** be kind to someone ☐   **b** be nasty to someone ☐

Presentation

2 **Warm up** Read the introduction to the article on page 53. What are some examples of bullying?

3 Read the article and answer the questions.

1 Where does a lot of bullying happen?
2 Which footballer was bullied at school?
3 What did bullies do to Taylor Swift?
4 Why do people bully?
5 What advice does the writer give to victims of bullying?

4 Read *Language focus*. <u>Underline</u> sentences with *where*, *which, who* and *that* in the article.

5 Study the examples in *Language focus* and complete the rules with *where*, *who* or *which*.

• Use .... or *that* with people.
• Use .... or *that* with things.
• Use .... with places.

6 ◉ 2.06 Ⓒircle the correct words. Then listen and check.

Language focus

• School should be a place **where** students feel safe.
• People **who** bully do it for different reasons.
• Most schools have lessons **which** help students talk about bullying.
• There are also internet sites and helplines **that** give advice.

We moved to a new town last year and I had to go to a new school, ¹ **where /** **which** I liked. I made new friends ² **who / which** were really nice. But there was a boy ³ **who / which** didn't like me. He waited for me in the park ⁴ **which / where** we hung out together. He said horrible things ⁵ **who / which** weren't true. It was an experience ⁶ **where / which** made me very unhappy. But I told my teachers, ⁷ **where / who** stopped the bullying. Now the boy has apologised to me.

Bullying
–it's NOT OK

Bullying. Saying horrible things to people, laughing at them, or sending nasty text messages. Refusing to talk to them or hurting them and damaging their things. It can happen because of your skin colour, your religion or your looks, because you are different, or even because you are a good student.

School should be a place where students feel safe. Unfortunately, it is also a place where bullying happens a lot. And students who are the victims of bullying feel frightened, lonely and depressed.

There are many famous people that were victims of bullying at school. Would you believe that bullying was a problem for David Beckham? The American singer Taylor Swift was also a victim of bullying and wrote a song about it. In the school canteen the bullies refused to eat with her. But when she became famous the girls who bullied her wanted her autograph!

People who bully do it for different reasons. They might want to look big or impress their friends, they might have personal problems, they might not know it is wrong. But that doesn't make bullying right, of course.

If you are the victim of bullying, or a friend of a victim, don't try to fight back on your own. You can talk to a teacher who you know, or tell your parents. And don't answer nasty text messages. You can report rude comments on social networking sites to internet providers and phone companies can block callers, and most schools have lessons which help students talk about bullying. There are also internet sites and helplines that give advice. So you are not alone!

Your Space   Talking about life

7   **Complete the sentences for you.**

- A place where I feel happy is …
- A person who I admire is …
- A singer who I like is …
- A thing which I carry with me is …
- A gadget which I want to buy is …

8   **Work in pairs. Compare your answers. Explain your reasons.**

A place where I feel happy is my bedroom. All my things are there, and I listen to music. And I sleep, of course!

Relative pronouns

1 **Read the rules and complete the cartoon with the words in the box.**

where   who   which

That's the bike *which* I bought my son for his birthday. That's the shop *where* I bought it. And that's the man *who* sold it to me.

Use a defining relative clause to say exactly which person, place or thing you mean.

		Pronoun	
People	Ben is the boy	**who / that**	made the school website.
Things	This is the photo	**which / that**	I took yesterday.
Places	The city	**where**	I was born is beautiful.

2 (Circle) **the correct relative pronoun.**

1 Where are the CDs *who /* (*which*) were on the bookcase?

2 I think it's going to rain. Do you have an umbrella *that / where* I can take with me?

3 I don't like the painting *which / who* my parents bought last week.

4 I've already met the boy *who / where* is sitting next to Jason.

5 James found the book *who / that* you left here.

6 I've seen a spaceship *where / which* has flown to the moon.

7 I got a text message from the girl *where / that* I met in Rome.

8 This is the only bag *that / where* I want to take on the plane.

3 ⊙ **2.07 Complete the problems with** *which*, *who* **or** *where*. **Then listen and check.**

File   Edit   View   Go   Bookmarks   Tools   Help
search   Subscrib

1 I've got a kid brother ....*who*.... always hangs out with me and my friends. He's so annoying.

2 I wanted an electric guitar for my birthday. But my parents bought me one .... isn't very good.

3 I hate going shopping with my mum. She takes me to shops .... she buys her clothes.

4 The town .... I live is so boring. There's nowhere to hang out.

5 My friend is a person .... just wants to have fun. How do I tell her I think studying is important?

6 I failed an exam .... was really important for my future. My parents are angry.

4 ✎ **Work in pairs. Write a piece of advice to each person in Exercise 3.**

1 Perhaps your brother wants to spend some time with you. Do something that he likes. Why not go to the park with him and play football?

5 ✎ Write ten sentences about you, your friends and family using these words.

> I   my dad   my best friend
> my mum   my uncle   my aunt
> my brother   my sister

⬇

> people   houses   food   films   books
> computer games   sports   music
> paintings   cars   holidays   school trips

⬇

> funny   unfriendly   exciting   boring
> relaxing   serious   easy   difficult
> noisy   quiet   traditional   modern
> old   new   hot   cold   spicy
> frightening   friendly   dangerous

> I like people who are funny.
> My dad likes food which is spicy.
> My best friend loves sports which are frightening.

6 🗩 Work in groups. Play the Definitions Game. Follow the instructions.

THE DEFINITIONS GAME

- Choose a person, a thing, or a place.
- Write a definition of the word (but don't say the word).
- Take it in turns to read your definitions.
- The first student to guess the word wins a point.

A It's a person who works in a garage.
B It's a mechanic.

B It's a place where you can see lots of animals.
C Is it a zoo?

C It's a book which has lots of definitions.
D A dictionary.

➡ **Language check page 130**

Word chunks

Some groups of words are used every day in conversation. They are called *chunks*.

7 <u>Underline</u> these *chunks* in the conversation.

I don't know	I think it's	you have to
do you want	a lot of	and it was
I don't think	do you know	

Jacob What <u>do you want</u> to do this evening?
Carla I don't know.
Jacob Well, there are a lot of good films on at the cinema.
Carla Do you know which ones?
Jacob Um, there's the new James Bond film. I think it's on at the Odeon.

Carla I don't think I've ever seen a James Bond film!
Jacob You're joking! I love them. I saw the last one three times and it was really good. But we can choose a different film if you prefer.
Carla No, that's fine. When shall we meet?
Jacob The film starts at six, so you have to be at the cinema at quarter to six.

8 Complete the sentences with these words.

> have   lot   ~~think~~   know   want   was   you   don't

1 **Sara** What's the time?
   Eren I ____think____ it's five o'clock.
2 We're late. I _____ think we're going to get there on time.
3 There are a _____ of problems on this website.
4 Listen class, you _____ to study hard this year.
5 **Dad** Where are my trainers?
   Mum I'm sorry, I don't _____ .
6 I had a tuna sandwich for lunch and it _____ delicious.
7 **Chris** Do _____ know why the bus has stopped?
   Tony No idea!
8 Who do you _____ to invite to your party?

Reading and speaking

1 **Warm up** Work in groups. Discuss the things that we need to live. Are these things essential (*E*) or non-essential (*NE*)?

water ☐   newspapers ☐   shoes ☐   a home ☐   paper and pens ☐   TV ☐
food ☐   family jewellery ☐   radio ☐   books ☐   toys ☐   electricity ☐
music ☐   mobile phones ☐   love ☐   make-up ☐   medicine ☐   respect ☐
vaccinations ☐   clothes ☐   education ☐   dance ☐   games ☐   computers ☐

2 Read the article and complete the headings with these words.

~~water~~   education   health   a home   food

DIFFERENT LIVES – SAME RIGHTS!

There are millions of children and teenagers in the world. And each one has rights – it doesn't matter who they are, what sex they are, where they live or what they believe in. There is a special agreement between almost every country in the world called the United Nations Convention on the Rights of the Child, which promises these rights to the world's young people.

The right to ...

Water

Millions of people don't have clean water or they have to walk a long way to get it. Water is essential to life and everyone should have safe water near their home.

There are all sorts of homes – houses, flats, tents. Having a home is a right, and it should be a place where every young person feels safe, protected and comfortable.

Without food we would die. But unfortunately many people are starving. Everyone should have enough to eat so they can develop properly.

PROTECTION

Everyone needs a person who loves and cares for them and gives them a family life. Young people need someone to give them food, buy them clothes and love them.

AN IDENTITY

We all have the right to a name and nationality. We should also be free to say what we believe, get information freely and learn about our culture.

People around the world die because they haven't got medicine or vaccinations. Everybody should have access to doctors and hospitals. And if a child is disabled, adults should help them to achieve as much as possible.

A basic right for young people is the chance to go to school. It's not fair that some young people don't get an education and have a good future life.

A CHILDHOOD

Millions of 5 to 14 year-olds work long hours. It is wrong that they don't have a childhood and can't play. This is an important part of growing up.

3 **Work in pairs. Read the article again and discuss the questions.**

- Why is water important? What do we use it for?
- What happens if we don't get enough to eat?
- Who gave you your name? Why is it important to have a name?
- How does school help you to prepare for the future?
- What sort of work is it OK for a teenager to do in your country?

Listening and writing

4 **◉ 2.09** **Listen and choose the best sentence (A or B) about each person.**

1 **A** Nadine stopped going to school when she was 11. She has to work at home but her brothers go to school.

B Nadine goes to school and she is learning to read and write. She plays outside a lot with her friends.

2 **A** Paulo doesn't go to school. He lives on the street and sells ice cream. He would like to go to school and have a family.

B Paulo doesn't go to school. He works on a rubbish dump. He has a family and a nice home.

3 **A** Anita can't walk or play outside. She wants to be a teacher but she doesn't like studying.

B Anita had polio. She couldn't walk. She had an operation. Now she can walk and she goes to school. She wants to be a doctor.

Study skills

Be prepared
Before you listen, read the questions because they give you information. For example, you know Nadine will talk about school, her family and work or play.

---

5 **Work in pairs. What do you think should change in these young people's lives?**

Nadine should go to school. She shouldn't have different opportunities from her brothers. She shouldn't have to work so hard at home.

6 **Write about four things you like about your life. Explain your reasons. Choose from:**

> family   home   free-time activities   school   friends   home town   possessions

I love my family. My mum and dad are great fun. My dad's jokes are terrible and my mum makes me tidy my room but I don't mind! I've got an older brother and we play football.

6A She said she was living her dream

Vocabulary • Talent show

1 🔘 **2.13** **Match the words with the pictures. Then listen and check.**

viewers [3]   judges [ ]   finalists [ ]   presenter [ ]

winner [ ]   audience [ ]   contestants [ ]

Presentation

2 **Warm up** **Work in pairs. Discuss the questions.**

Do you ever watch talent shows on TV? Why? / Why not?
Which performers have become famous from these programmes?

3 🔘 **2.14** **Listen and read the interview on page 59. Then answer the questions.**

1 Where did Sophie interview the finalists?
2 What does Jasmine like about the competition?
3 Who does Theo get a lot of support from?
4 Why do you think this is Reuben's last chance to become famous?
5 Why does Lisa like Jasmine?
6 Who decides the result of the final?

4 **Read *Language focus*. Find the sentences in the text on page 59.**

5 **Match the statements with the people.**

~~Jasmine~~ Theo Lisa Max Reuben

1 (I'm having a fantastic time.)   *Jasmine*

2 (The result doesn't depend on me.)

3 (I talk to my parents every day and they give me a lot of support.)

4 (I'm a great fan of Jasmine because she always gives 110 per cent.)

5 (I'm not going to waste it.)

Language focus

• Theo **said** he **was** very nervous.
• She **told me** she **loved** everything about the show.
• He **said that** he **was working** very hard.
• Max Callow **told me that** he **was** really looking forward to Saturday.

2.14

Pop Star
the final

Lisa

Max

Reuben

Jasmine

Theo

On Saturday, 20 million viewers will watch the final of this year's Pop Star competition. Sixteen contestants took part in the first round of Pop Star but now there are only three left! And soon we will know the name of the winner. Sophie Devine met the three finalists at a secret location outside London. They told her about their hopes – and their fears.

First of all, I spoke to 22-year-old **Jasmine**. She told me she loved everything about the show. She said she liked being with the other contestants and she enjoyed learning new dances. She said she was living her dream. Jasmine told me that she was having a fantastic time.

Then I chatted with **Theo**. This shy and polite 16-year-old student is the favourite to win. Theo said he was very nervous. He told me he talked

to his parents every day and they gave him a lot of support. Theo said that he was going to give the best performance of his life.

Finally, I spoke to 28-year-old **Reuben**. He said that he was working very hard. He said he got up at five o'clock every morning and then rehearsed all day. He told me that this was his last opportunity to become famous. He wasn't going to waste it!

I also met two of the judges. What were their thoughts about this year's finalists?

Lisa Lux said they had three great singers this year. Lisa said she was a great fan of Jasmine because she always gave 110 per cent. She told me that Jasmine had a lot of talent and ambition.

Max Callow told me that he was really looking forward to Saturday. He told me that he wasn't being rude but he didn't think Theo had a chance. But he said the result didn't depend on him. The viewers had the final vote!

Watch the Pop Star final on Saturday, and don't forget to call and vote!

Your Space   Giving opinions

6   2.15   Listen to Reuben, Jasmine and Theo and decide who should win the Pop Star final.

7   Work in groups. Discuss the performances and decide on a winner.

A I think Reuben should win. He's got the best voice.
B I don't agree. I think Jasmine should win because …
C No, I think …

Reported speech – statements

1 **Look at the rules and the table. Then complete the sentences.**

- We often use *that* in reported speech. But you can omit it.

  I've got a headache ⟶ *He said (that) he had a headache.*

Direct speech	Reported speech
Present simple	**Past simple**
Molly said, 'I **drink** coffee.'	Molly said that she **drank** coffee.
am/are/is	***was/were***
Dan said, 'I**'m** cheerful.'	Dan said that he **was** cheerful.
has/have got	***had***
Sarah said, 'I**'ve got** a sore throat.'	Sarah said that she **had** a sore throat.
Present continuous	**Past continuous**
Harry said, 'Dad **is working**.'	Harry said that Dad **was working**.
am/are/is going to	***was/were going to***
Chris said, 'I**'m going to** watch a film.'	Chris said that **he was going to** watch a film.

- These are common pronoun and possessive adjective changes.

I ⟶ he/she   we ⟶ they
my ⟶ his/her   our ⟶ their
me ⟶ him/her   us ⟶ them

1

Henry's got a bag over his head!

He doesn't like horror films.

Lisa said that Henry .... a bag over his head.

Melanie said that he .... horror films.

2

There are two sharks!

We aren't going in the sea!

Leo said there .... two sharks in the sea!

Rosie said they .... in the sea.

2 **Report what the friends said.**

1 Lukas has a new mobile phone.   Elizabeth said that Lukas …

2 We're going to the cinema.   Stephen said that they …

3 Olivia sits next to me in class.   Jade said that Olivia …

4 I've got three guitars!   Matthew said that he …

5 I'm going to visit my gran on Sunday.   Simon said that he …

6 I'm very hungry.   Nicola said that she …

3 ⊙ **2.16** **Listen and report what Ben and Maria say.**

Ben said that he felt tired.

4 ⭐ **Work in pairs. Tell your partner four things about you. Then report your partner's sentences to the class.**

I play … I don't play …

I listen to … I like …

I don't listen to … I don't like …

Juan said that he liked chocolate ice cream.

5 ⊙ **2.17 Listen and match the statements with the people.**

THE BRIGHTEST STARS IN TENNIS

This week I meet the new tennis sensation, brother and sister Jonas and Justine!

A B

"We train every day for seven hours." A

"Playing tennis isn't always exciting!" ☐

"I also go running and work out in the gym." ☐

"We have got lots of titles and prizes." ☐

"We are brother and sister and best friends, too." ☐

"We argue sometimes!" ☐

"We get on very well." ☐

"We don't go out very much because we don't have time." ☐

"We are both studying for our school exams." ☐

6 🖊 **Report the quotes in Exercise 5.**

Justine said they trained every day for seven hours.

7 **Imagine you are a famous person, for example a pop star, film star or sportsperson. Answer these questions.**

- What do you do?
- Where are you from?
- How old are you?
- What's your daily routine?
- What are your future plans?
- What do you like about your job?
- What don't you like?

8 ⭐ **Work in pairs. Use the questions and answers from Exercise 7. Take turns to interview each other. Take notes from the interview.**

 Get it right!

Reporting verbs: say/tell

- When you want to mention who the listener is, use *tell* + name/pronoun.

Pete **told me** that he liked Robert Pattinson. NOT ~~Pete said me that he liked Robert Pattinson.~~

- Use *say* when you don't mention the listener.

She **said** she was going home.

9 🖊 **Write a news report about the interview in Exercise 8.**

Ricardo is a famous football player. He's from Barcelona. He told me that he played for Real Madrid …

Soundbite

/uː/ /ʊ/

A ⊙ **2.18 Listen and repeat.**

1 do food blue crew movie
2 put good look hood should

B ⊙ **2.19 Listen and decide if each word sounds like group 1 or 2 in Exercise A.**

cook 2 choose ☐ pull ☐ book ☐
hood ☐ drew ☐ sugar ☐ pool ☐

Grammar
reported speech – modals, *yes/no* questions
Functions
talking about films • reporting

Vocabulary • Making a film

1 🔘 **2.20** Match the beginnings of the sentences with the endings. Then listen and check.

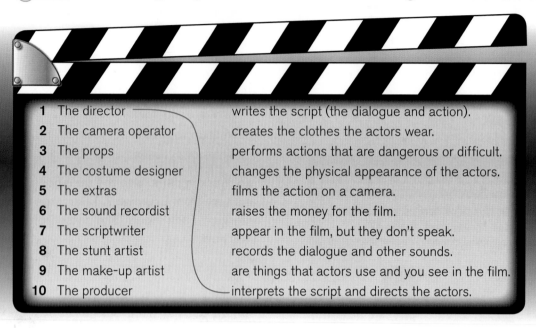

1	The director	writes the script (the dialogue and action).
2	The camera operator	creates the clothes the actors wear.
3	The props	performs actions that are dangerous or difficult.
4	The costume designer	changes the physical appearance of the actors.
5	The extras	films the action on a camera.
6	The sound recordist	raises the money for the film.
7	The scriptwriter	appear in the film, but they don't speak.
8	The stunt artist	records the dialogue and other sounds.
9	The make-up artist	are things that actors use and you see in the film.
10	The producer	interprets the script and directs the actors.

Presentation

2 **Warm up** Work in pairs. Read and answer the questions in the webzine introduction on page 63.

3 🔘 **2.21** Listen and read the interview and article. Then answer the questions.

1 What is Lauren doing in the film?
2 Where has she got the film equipment from?
3 Why doesn't she want to be a professional director?
4 What does Lauren want to do in the future?
5 What kind of film is she making?
6 Why did she call her film *What am I doing here*?

4 **Read *Language focus*. Then underline the other reported questions in the webzine.**

5 🔘 **2.21** Listen to the interview again and underline Nathan's direct questions.

6 **Write Nathan's questions. Put the words in the correct order.**

1 she filmed / I asked if / at the weekend
  I asked if she filmed at the weekend.
2 it was easy / to make a film / I asked if
3 I asked if / after school / Lauren worked
4 her main actor was / I asked if / in her class at school
5 very stressed / she was feeling / I asked if
6 she wanted / I asked if / to go to Hollywood

Language focus

• **I asked if it was** expensive to make a film.
• **I asked Lauren if she acted** in the film.

A

Have you ever wanted to make a film?
Have you ever dreamed of going to Hollywood?
Do you want to be an actor?
Would you like to make a film?
Then check out student Lauren Chapman.
She and her friends are making their dreams come true!

B

Nathan It's great to meet you, Lauren. Are you the director of the film?

Lauren Yes, I am. I'm the scriptwriter, too.

Nathan Wow, I'm impressed! Do you act as well?

Lauren No way! I can't act! But I'm working with some great actors.

Nathan Is it expensive to make a film?

Lauren Yes, it is. But this is a school project and we're using the school camcorder and computer.

Nathan Do you want to become a professional director?

Lauren No, not really. There's too much stress. A director has to think about too many things. But I love writing. I want to be a scriptwriter!

Nathan Are you planning to make other films?

Lauren Yes, I am. But we have to finish this film first! We'll finish it before the end of term. That's the important thing!

C Lauren Chapman is still only 14, but she's the writer and director of a film comedy called *What am I doing here?* Let's find out more.

I asked Lauren if she acted in the film. She told me that she couldn't act but she was working with some fantastic actors. I asked if it was expensive to make a film and she said it was. However, she said it was a school project and they were using school equipment. Then I asked if she wanted to become a professional director. She said that she didn't, but she wanted to be a scriptwriter.

I asked her if she was planning to make other films. She said she was, but she had to finish this film first! Then she told me about the plot of her film. The main character is a girl with a big problem. She wakes up one morning and doesn't know where she is. She doesn't recognise anybody around her. She doesn't even remember her own name!

Your Space   Talking about films

7   Think about the last film you saw at the cinema or on TV.
Note any details you can remember.

Film: The Karate Kid, Actors: Jackie Chan, Jaden Smith

8   **Work in groups. Talk about your films.**

A The last film I saw was *The Karate Kid*.
B Who was in it?
A Jaden Smith was the Karate Kid, Jackie Chan was the teacher.
C Was it exciting?

Chat zone

check out
I'm impressed!
not really

Reported speech – modals

1 Look at the table. Then complete the sentences.

Direct speech	Reported speech
can	*could*
Jack said, 'I **can** play the piano.'	Jack said he **could** play the piano.
will	*would*
Ross said, 'I **will** go to university when I am older.'	Ross said he **would** go to university when he was older.
must / have to	*must / had to*
Megan said, 'We **must** eat fruit.'	Megan said that they **must** eat / **had to** eat fruit.
Harry said, 'I **have to** go to the dentist.'	Harry said he **had to** go to the dentist.
mustn't	*mustn't*
The steward said, 'You **mustn't** use your mobile phones.'	The steward said that we **mustn't** use our mobile phones.

1 (I can't swim.)

Ross said he <u>couldn't swim</u> .

2 (You must do all these exercises.)

Mr Mitchell said we ....

3 (I have to go to the shop on the way home.)

Mum said she ....

4 (Temperatures will go up in the next 20 years.)

Scientists said temperatures ....

5 (I won't pass the exam.)

Alina said she ....

6 (Leon can't ride a bike!)

Leon's brother said Leon ....

7 (You mustn't walk on the grass.)

The man said we ....

8 (Alex won't get to the party on time.)

Ruth said Alex ....

2 📖 Read the interview and complete the article.

Abi So, are you going to win an Oscar, Scott?

Scott I won't win the Oscar, but I'm sure that the film will win!

Abi What have you learnt from your time in the Amazon?

Scott My limitations! I can do white-water rafting, but I can't climb mountains.

Abi Do you do your own stunts then?

Scott No, I don't do my own stunts! There's a brilliant stunt artist.

Abi What about your private life?

Scott I'm going to marry Zoe Foster. She's the love of my life.

Abi What will you do next, Scott?

Scott It'll be a film about the Antarctic! But I have to get the money first.

Scott Gibson, the star of the new film *Lost in the Amazon*, was in Hollywood for the Oscars.

He said he [1] <u>wouldn't win</u> an Oscar but that he [2] .... that the film [3] ....
He told us about his experience in the Amazon. He said that he [4] .... white-water rafting but that he [5] .... mountains.
He told us that he [6] .... his own stunts because there [7] .... a brilliant stunt artist.
We have hot news! He told us that he [8] .... marry Zoe Foster. He said that she [9] .... the love of his life! How romantic!
And what are Scott's plans for his next film? He said that it [10] .... a film about the Antarctic. He said that he [11] .... the money first.
Good luck, Scott!

Reported speech – *yes/no* questions

To report *yes/no* questions, follow these rules.

- Use *asked + if.*

  Are you hungry? ⟶ *He **asked if** I was hungry.*

- Use the positive verb order.

  Is   it   Monday?

  She asked if **it   was**   Monday.

3 Complete the reported questions with the correct verbs.

1 'Are they English?'

 She asked if they ....*were*........ English.

2 'Do you speak Spanish?'

 He asked if I .... Spanish.

3 'Does your dog bite?'

 The postman asked if my dog ....

4 'Do you feel ill?'

 Amber asked if I .... ill.

5 'Do they often cycle to school?'

 He asked if they often .... to school.

6 'Are you leaving?'

 My friend asked if I ....

4 ⊙ **2.22** Listen to the questions and quickly write your answers.

5 ☆ Work in pairs. Take turns to report the questions you heard. Then compare your sentences with your partner.

 The woman asked if I spoke Spanish.

6 ☆ Work in pairs. Write four questions, starting with *Is, Are, Do* or *Does*.

 Is your brother 12 years old?
 Do you have a garden?

7 ☆ Work in groups. Ask and answer the questions. Make notes of all the questions and answers. You only have three minutes!

8 Now report the questions and answers to the class.

 Arun asked Tim if his brother was 12. He said that his brother wasn't 12, he was seven.

⇨ **Language check page 130**

take

Paul **took part** in a talent show in New York.

He **took** a very big rucksack and his guitar.

He **took** a train to the airport.

At security he **took off** his hat.

The plane **took off** five hours late.

The journey **took** four hours.

The show **took place** in a TV studio.

After the show they **took** photos of him.

9 Complete the sentences with the correct form of *take*.

1 We waited for 30 minutes on the runway. Finally the plane ....*took off*.... .

2 Where does this evening's concert .... ?

3 The best way to get to London from here is to .... a train.

4 My house is close to school. It only .... ten minutes on foot.

5 You look hot. Why don't you .... your coat?

6 I think it's going to rain. Don't forget to .... an umbrella!

7 Would you like to .... in an art competition?

8 I've just .... some brilliant photos on my holiday.

Reading and listening

1 **Read the article quickly. Then match the jobs with the paragraphs.**

a Runner **b** Prop maker **c** Make-up artist **d** Driver **e** Editor
f Creature maker **g** ~~Costume maker~~ **h** Visual effects artist **i** Caterer

ACTION!
BEHIND THE SCENES
AT THE MOVIES!

▶▶▶ You're at the cinema. At the end of the film, do you leave while the credits are on? Next time, why don't you stay and read the names? They tell you about the hundreds of people who worked on the film. Here are just a few!

1 _Costume maker_
Costume makers make or find all the clothes, shoes, hats and jewellery that actors wear – from historical to modern day or futuristic! They can take months to make.

2
These people can make a young actor look older, or make a human into an alien! Sometimes they use extra body parts which can take many hours to complete!

3
There are hundreds of objects in films. Tables, beds, phones, even trees! Prop makers are very artistic and have to have lots of practical skills.

4
These designers make models of monsters, dinosaurs, aliens and body parts which are incredibly realistic and can move.

5
Film crews work long hours and they eat a lot of food too. Catering staff cook and serve delicious breakfasts, lunches, dinners and snacks from inside trucks!

6
Most filming is on location, and drivers transport equipment, props, mobile offices, caravans on big trucks! Everything and everyone must arrive at exactly the right time.

7
To make a film, someone has to do the photocopying and take messages! Being a runner is the first job for many people in the film industry!

8
Teams of computer graphics artists take many months to make the animations. It can take ten hours to make just ten seconds of effects!

9
After filming is finished there is still lots to do! In the studio, editors choose what film to use and add special effects, graphics, sound and music. This stage creates the final film.

2 Read the article again and put the jobs in these groups.

costume maker

before filming

during filming

after filming

3 Write the names of the jobs. Sometimes more than one is possible.

Who ...
1 makes things?   3 works with computers?   5 works in a studio?
2 makes food?   4 drives?   6 runs around?

4 ⊙ 2.24 Listen and match the speakers with the jobs. There are two extra jobs.

Write *1*, *2* or *3*.

Prop maker ☐   Creature maker ☐   Make-up artist ☐   Editor ☐   Runner ☐

5 ⊙ 2.24 Listen again. Are the sentences true (*T*) or false (*F*)?

1 Jordan said she was 20 years old.   F
2 She did the make-up for the *Twilight* movies.
3 Gabriel studied very hard to learn to do his job.
4 He thinks the best thing he has made is a mechanical crocodile.
5 Rosie works long hours and doesn't get a lot of money.
6 She does the same things every day.

Study skills

Getting the gist
You don't have to understand everything – key words are enough. To identify the creature maker, listen for words like *make*, *move*, *monsters*, *creatures* and *animals*.

Speaking and writing

6 Read the questions and make a note of your answers.

My future career

1 What are you good at? What are you interested in?

2 What subjects would you like to study when you have to specialise? Do you need those subjects for your future career?

3 What job would you like to do when you finish your education? Do you need to get qualifications to do that job?

7 Work in groups. Discuss the questions from Exercise 6.

A My favourite subject is English. What's yours?
B Mine is PE. I'm good at sport.

8 Write three paragraphs about your future.

 Communication page 113   **Your Space Web Zone**

Grammar
second conditional – statements, questions and short answers

Functions
talking about imaginary situations

Vocabulary • Crime

1 ◉ 2.28 **Complete the sentences with the type of criminal. Then listen and check.**

> burglar   pickpocket   shoplifter   vandal   ~~thief~~   mugger

1 A _thief_ is a person who steals things.
2 A _____ is a person who attacks you in the street and takes your money, mobile phone, etc.
3 A _____ is a person who steals things from shops.
4 A _____ is a person who breaks into houses and steals things.
5 A _____ is a person who steals things from pockets and bags.
6 A _____ is a person who damages public property.

2 **Work in pairs. Discuss the questions.**

Which crimes are the most serious / least serious?
Which criminals are the most dangerous?

Presentation

3 **Warm up** **Quickly read the questions on page 69. Which activities are crimes from Exercise 1?**

4 ◉ 2.29 **Listen to Megan and Henry doing the questionnaire. Make a note of Megan's answers. Then add up the a's and b's and read her score. Is she a good citizen?**

5 **Work in pairs. Do the questionnaire on page 69 together. What's your score?**

6 **Read *Language focus*. Then underline other examples of *if* sentences on page 69.**

Language focus

• **If** your friend **dropped** litter in the street, **would you say** something?
• **Yes**, I **would**.
• **No**, I **wouldn't**.
• **If** a shop assistant **gave** me too much change, I **would give** it back.

7 **Match the beginnings of the sentences with the endings.**

1 If I had a camera,
2 If your mum saw your room,
3 If Alex went to the gym,
4 If I went to Egypt,
5 If we lived in the country,
6 If you trained your dog,

a it wouldn't run away.
b we would have a bigger garden.
c he wouldn't feel so unfit.
d she would be very angry.
e I would visit the Pyramids.
f I would take your photo.

Are you a good citizen?

1 If a group of new friends bullied someone at school, I would ...

  a keep quiet.
  b tell them to stop.

2 If I wanted to get into a pop concert I would ...

  a climb over the fence.
  b pay at the ticket office.

3 If a shop assistant gave me too much change, I would ...

  a keep it.
  b give it back.

4 If a friend stole money from his parents, I would ...

  a not say anything.
  b talk to him about it.

5 If a boy or girl said nasty things to me, I would ...

  a fight them.
  b walk away.

6 If your friend dropped litter in the street, would you say something?

  a No, I wouldn't.
  b Yes, I would.

7 If someone had an accident in the street, would you stop to help?

  a No, I wouldn't.
  b Yes, I would.

8 If one of your friends wanted to steal from a shop, would you help them?

  a Yes, I would.
  b No, I wouldn't.

9 If you saw an old person with heavy bags, would you offer to help?

  a No, I wouldn't.
  b Yes, I would.

SCORE

Add up the number of a's and the number of b's.

Mostly a's   Your actions sometimes have a bad effect on other people or are crimes! You should think before you act.

Mostly b's   You are a good citizen. You think about the impact your actions have on other people.

Your Space   Talking about imaginary situations

8 Complete the sentences for you.

  1 If I won a lot of money, I'd ...
  2 If I lived in New York, I'd ...
  3 If I saw a UFO, I'd ...
  4 If I had more time, I'd ...
  5 If I were famous, I'd ...

  1 If I won a lot of money, I'd build a sports club.

9 Work in groups. Compare your sentences.

Second conditional – statements

1 **Look at the pictures and write the correct results.**

> I would visit the Kremlin   she would be very scared   he would have more time

1

2

3

Condition	Result
If she saw a tarantula,	....
	....

Condition	Result
If he didn't play computer games,	....
	....

Condition	Result
If I went to Moscow,	....
	....

- Use the second conditional to talk about imaginary events.
- You can put the condition before or after the result.

  If I missed the bus, I would walk home.
  I would walk home if I missed the bus.

Get it right!

Only use *would* once in conditional sentences.

If we lived in a bigger house, I **would** have a bigger bedroom.

NOT ~~If we would live in a bigger house, I would have a bigger bedroom.~~

2 **Write sentences with the second conditional. Use the ideas below.**

1   I (live) in the UK

2   I (meet) my favourite pop star

3   I (hear) a strange noise at night

4   I (fly) in a helicopter

5   I (break) my leg

6   I (get) a part-time job

> not go outside to check   ~~speak really good English~~
> ask for an autograph   earn money for my holiday
> not play football for months   feel really excited

If I lived in the UK, I would speak really good English.

3 ⊙ **2.30** **Listen and (circle) the correct answers.**

Thinking about ME

1 I'd be happy if (my football team won) / I didn't have any homework.

2 I'd be nervous if   I had an exam / I was an actor in a play.

3 I'd have fun if   we went to the zoo / we went bowling.

4 I'd feel sad if   my hamster died / it rained for a month.

5 I'd be angry if   my friend told stories about me / a person hurt an animal.

6 I'd have a party if   I won some money / it was my birthday.

4 ✎ **Write sentences about you.**

I'd be happy if I met Beyoncé.

5 ☆ **Work in groups. Compare your ideas.**

Second conditional – questions and short answers

No, I wouldn't.

Would you buy a sports car if you had the money?

Yes, I would.

Remember! You can put the condition before or after the result.

Would you cycle to school if you had a bike?
If you had a bike, would you cycle to school?

6 Write the questions. Then match them with the answers.

1 you visit me / you come to my town?
Would you visit me if you came to my town?

2 Jack get better marks / he study more?
3 I be healthier / eat less chocolate?
4 Holly lose things / she tidy her room?
5 the room look better / I paint it blue?

a No, he wouldn't.   b Yes, you would.

c No, it wouldn't.   d Yes, she would.

e Yes, I would.

7 🗨 Work in pairs. Ask and answer the questions.

A Would you visit me if you came to my town?

B Yes, I would.

8 🔘 **2.31** Complete the questions in the questionnaire. Then listen and check.

How honest are you?

1 _Would you tell_ (you / tell) the truth if _your friend sang_ (your friend / sing) badly in a talent show? Y I N

2 If .... (you / find) your best friend's diary, ... (you / read) it? Y I N

3 If .... (you / not want) to go to school, ... (you / pretend) to be ill? Y I N

4 .... (you / tell) your dad if .... (you / break) his camera? Y I N

5 If .... (you / not like) your friend's new hair style, ... (you / say) it was great? Y I N

6 .... (you / look) if .... (your teacher / leave) the English test on her desk? Y I N

9 🔘 **2.31** Listen again and ⟨circle⟩ Lara's answers.

10 🗨 Do the questionnaire. Then discuss your answers with a partner. Give reasons.

A Would you tell the truth if your friend sang badly in a talent show?

B No, I wouldn't. I wouldn't want to upset her.

Soundbite

/ɪə/ /eə/

🔘 **2.32** Listen and say the chant.

We're here, we're there,
You can find us anywhere.
Act now, feel no fear,
Come and be a volunteer.
We care, we share,
Let's make things better everywhere.
Hear our voice, our message is clear,
Let's make this year a time to cheer. Hurray!

Grammar
second conditional – *wh-* questions *If ... were ...* , *a little / a few*

Functions
talking about politics

Vocabulary • Society

1   What's important to you? Choose three of the following things. Tell your class.

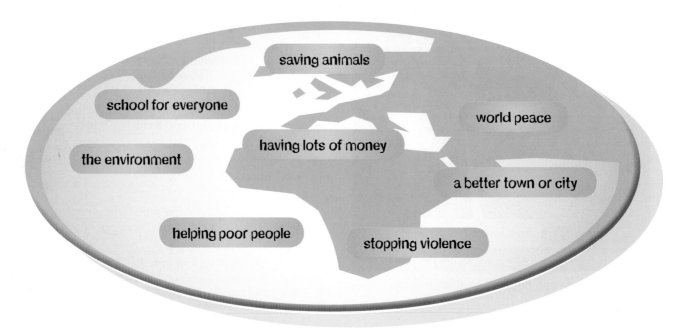

saving animals

school for everyone

world peace

having lots of money

the environment

a better town or city

helping poor people

stopping violence

Presentation

2   **Warm up** Read the webzine introduction on page 73. What questions are the Web Crew going to ask?

3   **2.33**   Read and listen to the webzine on page 73. Then answer the questions.

   1   Who is more concerned about the environment?
   2   Who does Aidan think earns too much money?
   3   Why does Maria think the voting age should change?
   4   What doesn't Aidan like about TV?
   5   Why does Maria think education is important?
   6   How does Aidan help a local charity?

4   Read *Language focus*. Then complete these sentences from the webzine.

   1   If I were a world leader, I .... pollution.
   2   If I were a world leader, I .... a law to cut advertising.
   3   If I were a rich pop star, I .... endangered species all around the world.
   4   If I were a rich pop star, I .... some fast cars!

Language focus
- **If** I **were** a world leader, I **would lower** the voting age to 16.
- **If** I **were** a rich pop star, I**'d spend** money on education.

5   Complete the sentences for you. Write two ideas for each sentence.
   If I were a world leader, I would ...
   If I were a rich pop star, I would ...

○ 2.33 We all want to make the world a better place. What would <u>you</u> do if you were a world leader? Would you make new laws? And if you were a millionaire, would you spend your money on good causes? Well, we asked you the questions, and here are some of the best answers!

What would you do if you were a world leader?

MARIA If I were a world leader, I would cut pollution. I'd encourage people to cycle and travel by bus. I'd also have a few car-free days every week.

AIDAN I'd pay nurses and doctors more money. Famous footballers and actors earn loads of money and people who do important jobs don't earn enough. And I'd phone all the world leaders and ask them to help me get rid of poverty.

If you were a world leader, what new laws would you introduce?

MARIA That's easy. If I were a world leader, I would lower the voting age to 16. I think young people should have a vote. Our opinions are important!

AIDAN Do you watch much TV? I only watch a few programmes because I think it's rubbish. There are too many advertisements. So if I were a world leader, I'd make a law to cut advertising. And I'd tell young people to stop watching TV all day. Do some sport, meet up with your friends. Get a life!

How would you spend your money if you were a rich pop star?

MARIA If I were a rich pop star, I'd spend money on education. The only way we're going to save the planet is by teaching people to change their habits. It's really important to help the environment. And if I were a rich pop star, I would protect endangered species all around the world.

AIDAN If I were a rich pop star, I'd buy some fast cars! But seriously, I'd give money to scientists so they can find a cure for terrible diseases. I sometimes give a little money to a local health charity, so I'd love to do more.

What would YOU do?
Add your comments and let us know!

Your Space   Talking about imaginary situations

6 Work in groups. If you started a new eco club at school, what would you do? Follow the instructions below.

Choose a name for your club and note three things that you would do, e.g.:
clean up the school • grow vegetables • collect money for charity •
recycle paper • put up bird boxes • plant trees • make art from rubbish

The Go-for-Green club

We would plant more trees.

7 Tell the class about your group's ideas.

Chat zone
loads of ...
I think it's rubbish!
Get a life!
But seriously, ...

Second conditional – *wh-* questions

What would you do if you lost your mobile phone?

I'd buy a better one!

Result		Condition
Where would you go	→	if you had a lot of money?
What would you do	→	if you found a burglar in your house?
Who would you go with	→	if you could take a friend on holiday?

1 Complete the questions with the verbs in brackets.

What would you do if ...

1 What would you do if you __had__ (have) a time machine?

2 Where would you go if you _____ (be) an explorer?

3 What book would you buy if your grandad _____ (give) you €20 to spend?

4 What would you eat if you _____ (go) to a restaurant tonight?

5 What would you do if you _____ (live) by the sea?

6 What would you do if you _____ (argue) with your best friend?

7 What would you do if you _____ (find) a burglar in your house?

8 What would you do if you _____ (meet) your favourite actor?

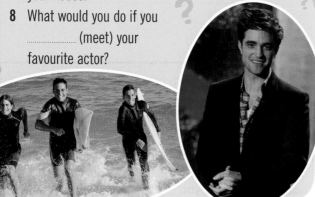

2 ⭐ Work in pairs. Ask and answer the questions.

A What would you do if you had a time machine?

B I'd travel into the future!

If ... were ...

If I were taller, I would become a champion basketball player.

3 Write answers to these questions. Give reasons.

1 If you were an animal, what would you be?
If I were an animal, I'd be a tiger because it is strong.

2 If you were a colour, what would it be?

3 If you were a car, what would you be?

4 If you were a vegetable, which one would you be?

5 If you were a famous person, who would you be?

a little / a few

4 Look at the rules and complete the sentences with *a little* or *a few*.

- Use *a little* with uncountable nouns to say a small amount.
  a little water
- Use *a few* with countable nouns to say a small number or not many.
  a few flowers

1

Thief   Give me your wallet!
Man   I've only got .... money.

2

Waiter   Anything else?
Amber   Just .... milk, please.

3

Keira   Did you enjoy the party on Saturday?
Tom   Not really. I only knew .... people.

4

Detective   What did you take from the shop?
Shoplifter   I only took .... DVDs.

5 ⭐ **Work in groups. Talk about the classroom. Use *a few*, *a little*, *a lot* and *not much*.**

| light | space | posters | pens | computers |
| water | students | noise | windows | paper |

▶ **Language check page 131**

Suffixes

We often make a noun for the job someone does by adding **-er/-or** to the end of the verb.

6 Match the words with the pictures.

designer [1]   cleaner [ ]   farmer [ ]
builder [ ]   director [ ]   sailor [ ]
author [ ]   conductor [ ]

Jobs

7 Match the words with the pictures.

cooker [8]   toaster [ ]   printer [ ]
stapler [ ]   lawn mower [ ]   can opener [ ]
coffee maker [ ]   dishwasher [ ]

Machines and gadgets

8 Write definitions for eight jobs, machines or gadgets.

1 A designer designs things such as clothes or books.
2 You cook food on a cooker.

Make a difference

Maybe you can't change the world. But you can make your school a nicer place.

What is a school council?

A school council is a group of students. Only students, no teachers or parents! Their aim is to make their school a nicer place for all the students in the school.

Are school councils new?

There have been school councils in the UK for over 40 years. In Ireland, Spain and Sweden, all state secondary schools have to have them.

Who is on a school council?

Students! Each year, every class elects two students to be members of the school council. In larger schools, each age group can have a separate school council, so a school in the UK may have up to seven different councils! The councils then have regular meetings where they discuss school life and make decisions.

What can school councils achieve?

'We've changed the design of our school canteen. We now sit at smaller tables. It's easier to chat with our friends so it's a lot quieter now.' *Ava, Broadway School, England*

'We now have recycling bins in the school for bottles and cans. That's good for the environment but it's good for our school, too. If we collect enough, our local government gives our school extra money!' *Harvey, Golden Hill School, New Zealand*

'We didn't like our old school uniform. We wore jackets and ties. But our school council had a better idea and now we wear sweatshirts. Cool!' *Sienna, International School, Spain*

'Our school council voted to start a steel band. So we raised money, bought the drums and had lessons. Last month we performed at a charity concert.' *Aidan, Willowbrook School, Ireland*

'People think teens are only interested in burgers and chips. But we introduced more healthy food to the lunchtime menu.' *Rebecca, Westland Academy, Scotland*

So do you want to make a difference? Well, why not set up a school council?

Reading and speaking

1 **Warm up** Look at the pictures on page 76 and read the heading. What do you think this article is going to be about?

2 **Read the article. Are the sentences true (*T*) or false (*F*)?**

1 A school council is a group of teachers, parents and students.   F
2 School councils started in the UK in the 1990s.
3 In Spain and Sweden state schools don't have to have school councils.
4 Each class votes for two students to be on the school council.
5 There can only be one council in a school.

3 **Read the article again and note what the school councils changed.**

Ava's school council changed the school canteen.

4 **Work in groups. Imagine you are going to set up a school council. Follow the instructions.**

• Think of improvements you would like to make to your school.
We believe our school should have better sports facilities.
• Choose one of your ideas and write a statement.
• Prepare a short talk about your idea.
• Give your talk to the class. Take a class vote on each idea.

Listening

5 **2.35 Listen and match the people with their concerns.**

1 Alex   a getting a job
2 Alice   b cultural tolerance
3 Mohammed   c the environment and endangered species
4 Yasmin   d cycling and not driving

6 **2.35 Listen again and complete the sentences.**

1 There are about .... endangered species in Arizona.
2 I know lots of .... people who are looking for ....
3 Cycle to school on the first .... in .... for the *International Walk and Bike to School Day*.
4 Over .... per cent of people in New Mexico are Hispanic, ... per cent are American Indians and .... per cent are from a German background.

Writing

7 **Write three paragraphs about <u>one</u> of these issues.**

a We should recycle more.
b We should cycle and walk more.
c We should ban plastic bags.

• Paragraph 1: write reasons why it is a good idea
• Paragraph 2: write reasons why it isn't a good idea or is difficult
• Paragraph 3: write your own opinions

Study skills

Paragraphs
Paragraphs are groups of sentences related to one idea. They make a text easier to read. They also help you to organise your ideas more clearly.

Grammar
present passive

Functions
talking about processes

Vocabulary • Irregular past participles

1 **◉ 2.38 Work in pairs. Write the past participles of the verbs. Then listen and check.**

write written   read   drink   eat   sing   win   lose   make

wear   speak   take   give   find   sell   put   do

Presentation

2 **Warm up Read the webzine introduction on page 79. Then discuss these questions. Make notes.**

What have you read this month? What have you written this month?
Read – a birthday card, a comic, school books
Written – an article for a sports website, a shopping list

3 **◉ 2.39 Listen and read the interview on page 79 and answer the questions.**

   1 What's the difference between a blog and a diary?
   2 Why does Holly like getting comments on her blog?
   3 Who reads Holly's blog?
   4 Why does Holly like reading other people's blogs?
   5 What can upset bloggers?

4 **Read *Language focus*. Then <u>underline</u> other examples of the passive in the interview on page 79.**

5 **Complete the sentences with past participles from Exercise 1.**

   1 English is _____spoken_____ in Australia.
   2 The *Twilight* novels are ____read____ by millions of people.
   3 *Happy Birthday* is ____sung____ on birthdays.
   4 Uniforms are ____taken____ at many schools.
   5 Plastic is ____made____ from petroleum.
   6 Tea is usually _____ with milk in Britain.

Language focus

- Blogs **are written** by all sorts of people.
- My blog **isn't read** by my 'real' friends.
- **Is** your blog **read** by a lot of people?

Your Space Talking about writing

6 **Work in groups. Discuss the questions.**

   • Do you keep a diary or write a blog?
   • How many text messages do you send in a week?
   • Do you chat with your friends on a social networking site?
   • Do you write poetry or stories?
   • Do you send postcards when you are on holiday?

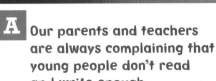
A Our parents and teachers are always complaining that young people don't read and write enough.
But are they being fair?

We think we're reading and writing a lot – we're just doing it in different ways from our parents.

For example, lots of young people don't write about their lives in diaries. They write blogs online. So this week Nathan talks to a very enthusiastic blogger. You know her already. It's Holly!

B **How is a blog different from a diary?**
Well, a diary is usually private. But with a blog, you can interact with other people – they read your blog and you read theirs.

Is your blog read by a lot of people?
Yes, it is. The number of visitors is recorded by a counter. But the best thing is when comments are posted. This means people find your blog interesting. And lots of photos are uploaded on our blogs, too. It's cool when a new blog is posted by one of your friends. You can see what they've done and what they're thinking about.

But who reads your blog, Holly? I've never seen it!
I know! That's why it's so great! My blog isn't read by my 'real' friends like you. It's read by my online friends. And when I write my blog I have a special name. This makes my blog sort of private and public at the same time!

Who are blogs written by?
Blogs are written by all sorts of people. Their age and interests are listed, so you can choose whose blogs to read. But, actually, I like going from blog to blog like a butterfly going to flowers, and reading about all sorts of lives. It helps me to understand more about people.

Have you ever had any problems on your blogsite?
Sometimes a nasty comment is posted. These are often anonymous. Bloggers are very upset by this – sometimes they are forced to close their blog. It's a sort of cyberbullying and I don't like it. But everyone is usually very friendly. I have a lot of online friends, and lots of advice, ideas and stories are shared on our blogs. It's fun!

Why don't YOU start a blog? Post your questions <u>here</u> and Holly will answer them!

Chat zone

sort of
actually
It's a bit like ...

Present passive – positive and negative

I	am		
he / she / it	is	taught	
you / we / they	are		

I	am	not	
he / she / it	is	not	taught
you / we / they	are	not	

- Use the passive when the action is more important than the person doing it.
  Mini Cooper cars **are made** *in Oxford.*
- You can say who does the action if it is important with *by*.
  Some vegetables at our school **are grown by** *the students.*

Get it right!

Remember to use the past participle when you form the passive, *not* the past simple.
New books are **written** every year.
NOT ~~New books are wrote every year.~~
Many different languages are **spoken** in our school.
NOT ~~Many languages are spoke in our school.~~

1 Complete the sentences. Write the correct form of the verbs in brackets.

WORLD FACT FILE

1. Mandarin Chinese _is spoken_ (speak) by nearly a billion people.
2. 1.7 million tonnes of seafood _is cooked_ (cook) every year in Spain.
3. More movies _are produced_ (produce) in India than in any other country.
4. 24.5 kilos of cheese _is eaten_ (eat) by every French person each year.
5. 70 per cent of the world's toys _is made_ (make) in China.
6. France _is visited_ (visit) by more tourists than any other country.
7. The game of cricket _are play_ (play) in the UK, Australia, South Africa and Asia.
8. More tea _is drunk_ (drink) in the UK than in any other country.

2 Complete the signs. Use the verbs in the box in the correct form.

print give serve repair use collect

1

ALL TYPES OF COMPUTER
are repaired
IN THIS STORE

2

Plastic rubbish
~~are~~ _is collected_
on Wednesday

3

While you wait!
Your photos
are printed
here in five minutes.

4
Change _is_ not _given_
by this drinks machine.

5

Only fresh ingredients
is used
to make our sandwiches

6

Breakfast _is served_
between 7 am and 10 am

3 Change these active sentences into passive ones.

1 A teacher opens the school gates at eight o'clock.
The school gates *are opened at eight o'clock* .

2 Some students play football before classes.
Football games *are played before classes* .

3 Our school recycles paper for charity.
Paper *is recycle by school* .

4 Each class writes articles for the school web magazine.
Articles *are written* .

5 My class uses the language lab a lot.
The language lab *is used by class* .

6 Many parents meet their children outside after school.
Children *are met* .

7 Students do exams in the main hall.
Exams *are done* .

8 Students and teachers eat lunch at 1.00 pm.
Lunch *is eaten* .

4 ✎ Work in pairs. Write passive sentences about your school.

Present passive – questions and short answers

Am	I		Yes, I am. No, I'm not.
Is	he / she / it	paid?	Yes, he / she / it is. No, he / she / it isn't.
Are	you / we / they		Yes, you / we / they are. No, you / we / they aren't.

Where	is	gold	found?
When	is	dinner	served?
How	are	these books	organised?
How often	is	this room	cleaned?

What	are	your shoes	made	of?
Who	is	this film	directed	by?

5 Put the words in the correct order to make questions. Then choose the best answers.

1 played / game / at Wembley / is / what / ?
a) football b) tennis
What game is played at Wembley?

2 penguins / at the South Pole / found / are / ?
a) yes b) no *Are penguins at the sou...*

3 are / tigers / where / found / ?
a) Asia b) Africa *where are tigers found*

4 born / Dalmatian dogs / are / with spots / ?
a) yes b) no *Are Dalmatian dogs born with spots*

5 made / is / how / ice? *How ice*
a) by freezing water b) by heating water

6 is / made of / what / ice cream / ?
a) milk, cream and sugar b) milk, cheese and sugar

7 the Olympic Games / held / are / how often / ?
a) every two years b) every four years

8 coffee / where / grown / is / ?
a) in about 50 countries b) in about ten countries

9 is / which food / found in / vitamin C / ?
a) meat b) fruit and vegetables

6 Work in pairs. Take turns to ask and answer the questions from Exercise 5.
A What game is played at Wembley?
B Football.
A That's right!

Soundbite

/e/ /eɪ/

A 2.40 Listen and repeat.
1 She waved goodbye when she left.
2 Every day energy is wasted in our homes.
3 I read a letter while I was on the train.
4 The pain in my leg was terrible!
5 I made a mistake about the date.
6 I haven't got any money, I spent it.

B 2.41 Listen and circle the words you hear.
1 get gate 3 met mate
2 wet wait 4 let late

8B Messages were sent ...

Grammar
past passive

Functions
speaking and listening
accurately

Vocabulary • Punctuation

1 ⊙ **2.42** **Match the words with the punctuation marks. Then listen and check.**

hyphen [f]   full stop / dot (in an email address) [e]   dash [h]   exclamation mark [g]
question mark [i]   colon [d]   capital letter [j]   apostrophe [c]   comma [a]   speech marks [b]

a (**,**)   b (**" "**)   c (**'**)   d (**:**)   e. **.**   f (**–**)   g (**!**)   h (**—**)   i (**?**)   j (**A**)

2 **Look at the article on page 83 and** (circle) **an example of each type of punctuation mark from Exercise 1. Is there one you can't find?**

Presentation

3 **Warm up** Quickly read the article on page 83 and match the paragraphs with the pictures.

4 ⊙ **2.43** **Listen and read the article again. Then match the years and the events.**

1 In 1876
2 In the 1830s
3 About 3,000 years ago
4 In the 1970s
5 In 20BC
6 In the 1800s
7 About 2,200 years ago

a letters were delivered by postmen.
b the Persians used horses to carry messages.
c people could phone and walk at the same time!
d flags were used to send messages.
e people spoke on a telephone for the first time.
f a special code was invented by Samuel Morse.
g birds carried the latest news.

5 **Read** *Language focus.* **Then** underline **other examples of the past passive in the article.**

6 **Complete the text with these words.**

> was seen
> were introduced
> ~~weren't recorded~~
> was played
> were recorded
> were transmitted
> was invented

Language focus

- Letters **were delivered** to people's homes.
- News **wasn't spread** quickly.
- Where **was** the postal service **invented**?

Do you remember videos?

These days, we can watch TV programmes when and where we want. But things were once very different ... Until the 1950s, TV programmes [1] weren't recorded in advance. They [2] were transmitted 'live'! This caused problems in the US because of different time zones. If a baseball match [3] was played at 9 pm in Los Angeles, it was midnight when it [4] was seen in New York! But in 1956, the video tape [5] was invented. After that, TV programmes [6]_____ and shown later. 20 years later, home video recorders [7]_____ and people could control what they watched and when they watched it.

Have you heard the news?

Communicating is easy – chatting, texting, surfing the web, exchanging news, photos, videos and music. But imagine a world without mobile phones and computers! How did people communicate?

◉ 2.43

1. Pigeon post

About 3,000 years ago, birds were used by the ancient Greeks. If you wanted the latest news from the Olympic Games, carrier pigeons were the quickest way to get it!

2. Horse power

Eight hundred years later, messages were carried across Persia and Egypt by men on horses. News wasn't spread quickly – but it only took ten days for a message to travel 3,000 kilometres.

3. Roman postmen

Where was the postal service invented? In ancient Rome in about 20BC! Just like today, letters were delivered to people's homes by postmen.

4. Flag waving

The ancient Greeks and Romans used flags to communicate. And in the early 1800s, flags were used again by the French navy. They could send 1,000 different messages!

5. Electrical revolution

Morse code – a system of dots and dashes – was invented by Samuel Morse in the 1830s. Morse used his code in the first telegraph message in 1837 – it only travelled three kilometres. But by 1886 a telegraph message was sent across the Atlantic Ocean.

6. On the phone

The first words were spoken on the phone by Alexander Graham Bell in 1876. He said, 'Mr Watson, come here. I want you!' But the telephone wasn't invented by just one person. The most important inventors were Antonio Meucci, an Italian, and Alexander Graham Bell, a Scottish-American.

7. The digital age

With computers the modern age of communication was born. The first emails were sent in the 1960s, but they weren't used much until the late 1980s. The first mobile phones in the 1970s weighed nearly a kilo and didn't work very well! Imagine that!

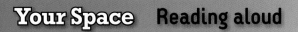

Your Space   Reading aloud

7 Look back through your Student's Book and choose a short paragraph from a reading text.

8 Work in pairs. Take it in turns to dictate your paragraph. Remember to give all the punctuation. Then compare your results.

Past passive

> My computer **was repaired** by my brother.

> The wheel **was invented** thousands of years ago.

I / he / she / it	was		paid.
you / we / they	were		

I / he / she / it	was	not	called.
you / we / they	were	not	

Was	I / he / she / it	told?
Were	you / we / they	

Yes, he / she / it was.	No, he / she / it wasn't.
Yes, you / we / they were.	No, you / we / they weren't.

Where	was	the car	left?
When	were	X-rays	invented?

---

1 Complete the news stories with the correct form of the verbs in the box.

| find   hit   arrest   ~~rescue~~   steal   remove |

1

Whale saves man

Diver Tamiki Ashida _was rescued_ by a tame whale in a diving contest.

2

CAKE THIEF

A lorry full of $40,000 worth of cheesecake .... by a thief who liked cakes.

3

Space boy

A boy .... by a meteorite from outer space.

4

Live salad!

Two green frogs .... in a salad. They were alive!

5

Wrong call

Two car thieves .... because they called the police when the car broke down.

6

BUZZING PLANE

10,000 bees .... from the wings of a plane!

2 🔘 **2.44** Listen to the radio news. Are the sentences true (*T*) or false (*F*)?

1 The diver, Tamiki Ashida, is a 63-year-old doctor.

2 The thief said that he wasn't ever going to eat cakes again.

3 Kyle Morris was walking home from school when the tiny meteorite hit him.

4 The frogs came from the Amazon and were taken to a zoo.

5 The police found $100,000 in a bag in the back of the car.

6 The plane was forced to land at Denver airport.

3 Complete the questions in the quiz with the correct form of the verbs in brackets.

WORDS WORDS WORDS

1 Where _was_ the first paper _made_? (make)
a Ancient Rome   b Ancient Egypt
c South America

2 When _was_ the first alphabet _____? (create)
a 1000BC   b 3000BC   c 200AD

3 Who _was_ it _invent_ by? (invent)
a The Ancient Egyptians   b The Phoenicians
c The Aztecs

4 Where _was_ the first European printing press _developed_? (develop)
a Germany   b Italy   c Denmark

5 When _was_ the internet _created_? (create)
a the 1970s   b the 1950s   c the 1980s

6 When _was_ the first text message _sent_? (send)
a 1997   b 1996   c 1993

7 What _was written_ in the first text message? (write)
a Happy Birthday   b Merry Christmas
c Happy New Year

4 Work in pairs. Ask and answer the questions. You must try to agree!

A Where was the first paper made?
B I'm not sure. I think it was made in Ancient Rome.
A I don't agree. I think the first paper was made in Ancient Egypt.

5 ◯ 2.45 Listen and check your answers.

6 Work in groups. Ask and answer questions.

A Were you born in October?
B Yes, I was! I was born on the 16th of October.

> born in October
> taken to a museum last year
> sent more than ten texts yesterday
> given a bike last year
> driven to school this morning

Language check page 131

Your words 8B

Sequencing

When we write, it is useful to show the stages in a process or the presentation of an argument. We use these words:

> Firstly • Secondly • Thirdly   Then • After that • Finally

7 Complete the article with the words above.

Aluminium cans are 100 per cent recyclable so don't forget to recycle them! But how is your empty can recycled?

F_irstly_, your drinks can and other rubbish is collected and taken to a recycling centre.
T_____ the rubbish is sorted and all the aluminium is separated.

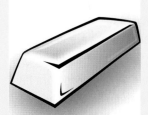

S_____, the cans are sent to a special factory. They are cut up into small pieces and cleaned.
A_____, they are melted down and turned into bars of aluminium.

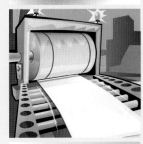

T_____, they are rolled into sheets of aluminium.

F_____, the aluminium sheets are used to make new products. The good news is that your old can becomes a new product in only six weeks!

8 Write a description of a process. You can use some of these ideas.

> making a cup of coffee   sending an email
>
> making a sandwich

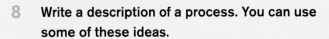

Reading and speaking

1 **Warm up** Work in pairs. Match the words with the pictures.

bow [5]   wave [ ]   shake hands [ ]   kiss [ ]   hug [ ]   point [ ]   touch [ ]   nod [ ]

2 Find and <u>underline</u> verbs from Exercise 1 in the article.

You don't need words!

Chatting, joking, texting, studying. We use language all the time. But we don't only communicate with words!

Animal language
Animals can't speak but they can communicate! Bees dance to tell other bees where flowers are, peacocks use their coloured feathers to find a mate, alligators hit the water with their tails, and whales sing across long distances.

You don't need words
Have you noticed how you can understand if your friends or family are happy or sad just by watching them? Our hands, our eyes, our faces, how we move, stand or sit all say a lot. We call this non-verbal communication.

Hundreds of gestures
Humans use hundreds of different gestures, including waving and pointing, to communicate. Some gestures, such as smiling, are universal, but others are cultural – we learn them from the people around us.

Don't be rude!
In many Asian countries it is rude to show the soles of your feet or touch someone on the head. And in countries such as England and Germany people don't touch very much if they aren't family or friends. It all depends where you are born.

Keep your distance!
Your personal space is the distance around you when you are with other people. Scientists have discovered that the distance varies a lot from country to country. For example, Americans usually like a larger personal space than many Europeans when they talk. This sort of cultural difference can cause problems!

Saying hello
There are many ways of saying hello. You can shake hands, wave, hug, bow, rub noses or kiss. In Japan people bow, and in Canada, the Inuit people rub noses. In many countries, people kiss to say hello, but there are rules about how many kisses and who you kiss. But some greetings are now international – like the hand shake, or the 'high five' hand greeting.

3 **Read the article. Are the sentences true (*T*) or false (*F*)?**

1 Animals are able to communicate with each other without words. T
2 Whales sing to communicate.
3 Non-verbal communication is when people speak different languages.
4 Smiling is a universal human gesture.
5 It is rude to show the soles of your feet in Europe.
6 It is usually polite to touch people's heads in Asian countries.
7 An American usually needs more personal space than a European.
8 A 'high five' is a way of saying hello.

4 **Work in groups. Discuss the questions. Tell the class about your group's answers.**

When you meet people for the first time, how do you greet them?
How do you greet your friends?   How do you greet members of your family?

Study skills

Using the internet
Use the internet to find out more about a new topic. You can get extra information and check facts. This will help you understand what you have read and improve your English.

Listening

5 **Look at the faces and match them with the emotions.**

disgust [b]   fear [ ]   surprise [ ]   anger [ ]   happiness [ ]   sadness [ ]

a   b   c

d   e   f

6 **3.03 Listen to the conversations and write the emotions.**

1 *anger*

Writing

7 **Write a short text about a time when you experienced one of the six emotions in Exercise 5. Include:**

- a title
- when and where it happened
- who you were with
- what happened
- how you felt

Mel lives in Cape Town, doesn't she?

Grammar
question tags – present simple positive

Functions
talking about a city

Vocabulary • Countries and cities

1 🔘 **3.06** **Match the flags with the countries. Then listen and check.**

a South Africa 8   **b** Brazil 2   **c** Mexico 6   **d** Japan 5   **e** India 4
f Turkey 9   **g** Australia 1   **h** China 3   **i** USA 10   **j** Russia 7

1

2

3

4

5

6

7

8

9

10

2 **Work in pairs. Match the cities with the countries in Exercise 1.**

1 Moscow 7   **2** Brasília 2   **3** Johannesburg 8   **4** Tokyo 5   **5** Washington 10
6 New Delhi 4   **7** Mexico City 6   **8** Canberra 1   **9** Istanbul 9   **10** Beijing 3

Presentation

3 **Warm up** **Look at the photos on page 89 and answer the questions.**

Who can you see in the photos? What do you think they are doing?

4 🔘 **3.07** **Listen and read the conversations on page 89. Are the sentences true (T) or false (F)?**

1 Samira wants to write an article about life in South Africa.
2 Johannesburg is on the coast.
3 Mel doesn't live in the suburbs.
4 She often goes to the skate park.
5 Her brother likes indoor go-karting.
6 It's time for Mel to have her breakfast.

5 **Read** *Language focus*. **Then complete the sentences with the tag questions. They all come from the conversations.**

1 You live in the suburbs, don't you ?
2 You can do some amazing tricks, can't you ?
3 And your brother likes indoor go-karting, doesn't he ?
4 It's time for your breakfast, doesn't it ?

Language focus

• Mel lives in Cape Town, **doesn't she?**
• It's on the coast, **isn't it?**

 3.07

A **It's Saturday – and Josh calls round to see Samira.**

Josh	Hey, what are you doing?
Samira	I'm going to talk to my friend Mel. I want to write about life in South Africa for the webzine.
Josh	Mel lives in Cape Town, doesn't she?
Samira	No, in Johannesburg.
Josh	Jo'burg? Oh right. It's on the coast, isn't it?
Samira	No way! It isn't by the sea. It's in the middle of the country!
Josh	Are you sure?
Samira	Of course I'm sure!
Josh	Hey, can I chat with Mel, too?
Samira	No problem.

B **Five minutes later …**

Samira	You live in the suburbs, don't you?
Mel	That's right. In Greenside. It's a lot nicer than the city centre! There are lots of trees and open spaces. And there's a big golf course – but I don't like golf!
Josh	Where do you hang out, Mel?
Mel	Well, I sometimes go to the shopping centres with my friends … but I go to the skate park a lot, too.
Samira	You can do some amazing tricks, can't you?
Mel	Yeah, well, they're quite good!
Samira	And your brother likes indoor go-karting, doesn't he?
Mel	You bet! He's the school champion!
Josh	It would be great to meet sometime, Mel.
Mel	I'd love to. But … sorry, guys, I have to go now.
Josh	It's time for your breakfast, isn't it?
Mel	You've got the time difference wrong, Josh. It's an hour later here! And I'm starving and I'm going to have my lunch!

Your Space   Talking about a city

6 **Complete the sentences about the capital city of your country.**

- The population is about …
- The most popular place for tourists is …
- The most beautiful building is …
- The ugliest building is …
- The tallest building is …
- The oldest part of the city is …

7 **Compare your ideas in groups. Do you agree?**

A The population is about five million, isn't it?

B I don't agree. I think it's only about three million.

Chat zone

No problem.
You bet!
I'm starving!

Question tags

- We use question tags when we think we know the answer.

statement	question tag
You**'re** English,	**aren't** you?
He**'s** got a goldfish,	**hasn't** he?
They**'re** eating dinner,	**aren't** they?
We **buy** that coffee,	**don't** we?
Matt **can** sail,	**can't** he?

You live here, **don't you**?

1 Match the question tags with the statements.

1 Mercury is the closest planet to the Sun, ⎡c⎤
2 You read a lot, ⬜
3 Ania has got a new guitar, ⬜
4 Penguins can swim, ⬜
5 There are eleven players in a football team, ⬜
6 Eric and Lucia are staying with their cousins, ⬜
7 Your mum's French, ⬜
8 They cycle home from school, ⬜
9 You've got two sisters, ⬜
10 You can do this exercise, ⬜

a aren't there?
b aren't they?
c isn't it?
d haven't you?
e don't you?
f isn't she?
g can't you?
h don't they?
i can't they?
j hasn't she?

2 Read the game rules and complete the conversation.

How to play the *Yes/No* Game
- **Each contestant has to answer ten questions.**
- **The contestant mustn't say yes or no!**

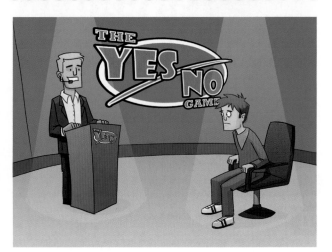

Larry Hello, and welcome to the *Yes/No Game*. And our first contestant is ... Ricky.

Ricky Hello, Larry.

Larry OK, the game starts ... now! Your name is Ricky, ...?

Ricky That's right.

Larry You live in Los Angeles, ...?

Ricky That isn't correct. I live in Seattle.

Larry Seattle? That's very cold in the winter, ...?

Ricky That is correct.

Larry You can swim, ...?

Ricky That's right. I like swimming.

Larry You've got a new sports car, ...?

Ricky Er, that's correct.

Larry You work with animals, ...?

Ricky That's right. I'm a vet.

Larry Your parents are sitting in the audience, ...?

Ricky Yes, they are.

Larry Oh, I'm so sorry, Ricky. You said yes!

3 🔘 **3.08** Listen and check. Then act out the conversation.

4 Work in pairs. Play the game. Use the ideas below or invent your own.

A You like swimming, don't you?
B That's right.

The Yes/No Game

- like swimming
- hate playing video games
- can play a musical instrument
- are fourteen
- play football
- read more than ten books a year
- have lots of homework
- watch TV every day
- are enjoying this game
- have got a pet
- have got a bike
- want to go home
- can speak English
- live in a house

Soundbite

Rising and falling intonation

A 3.09 Listen. Is the speaker sure (S) or unsure (U)?

1 Elena plays chess, doesn't she? ☐
2 Joe goes to my school, doesn't he? ☐
3 You play the guitar, don't you? ☐
4 You can swim, can't you? ☐
5 They've got a new car, haven't they? ☐
6 We have Maths tomorrow, don't we? ☐

B 3.09 Listen again and repeat with the same intonation.

5 Work in pairs. Write five things you think you know about your partner. Only use *have got*, the present simple or *can*. Use the phrases below or think of your own. Note if you are sure (S) or unsure (U).

doesn't play computer games | has a pet | can't swim | can play the piano | can play football | speaks Chinese | likes oranges | speaks French | likes music | likes chocolate | doesn't like fish

		sure/unsure
1		
2		
3		
4		
5		

6 Work in pairs. Ask and answer questions to check your ideas. Try to use the correct intonation.

A You live in a flat, don't you? (S)
B That's right.
B You can swim, can't you? (U)
A No, I can't!

7 Work in groups. Write six things you think you know about your teacher. Only use *have got*, the present simple or *can*. Note if you are sure (S) or unsure (U).

Mr Lopez is Mexican. U
He drives a red car. S

8 Ask your teacher the questions. Try to use the correct intonation.

A Can we ask you a question?
T Yes, of course. But I only answer polite questions!
A You're Mexican, aren't you?
T No, I'm not. I'm Canadian. But my parents are Mexican.

Grammar
question words ® • subject and object questions

Functions
talking about shopping centres and shopping

Vocabulary • Places in a town

1 Match the places with the reasons for visiting them.

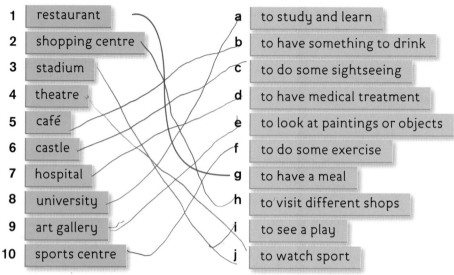

1	restaurant		a	to study and learn
2	shopping centre		b	to have something to drink
3	stadium		c	to do some sightseeing
4	theatre		d	to have medical treatment
5	café		e	to look at paintings or objects
6	castle		f	to do some exercise
7	hospital		g	to have a meal
8	university		h	to visit different shops
9	art gallery		i	to see a play
10	sports centre		j	to watch sport

2 Work in pairs. Make sentences about the places in Exercise 1.

You go to a restaurant to have a meal.

3 Work in pairs. Discuss the questions.

Are all of these places in your town? Are they in the town centre? Which ones do you often/never go to?

Presentation

4 **Warm up** Look at the article and photos on page 93. What do you think the article is about?

5 🔘 **3.10** Read and listen to the article. Then answer the questions.

1 When do the teens go to the shopping centre?
2 What do they do there?
3 What places and activities do they talk about?
4 Why do they think the shopping centre looks nice?
5 What would they change about the shopping centre?
6 Does Laura like going to the shopping centre all year?

6 Read *Language focus*. Then complete the questions with the verbs in the box.

go   sent   see   made

1 Who did you _see_ last weekend?
2 Who _made_ your breakfast this morning?
3 Where did you _go_ on your last holiday?
4 Who _sent_ you text messages last week?

Language focus

• **Who do** you **meet** here?
• **Who likes** shopping centres?
• **What do** you **do** here?

7 Work in pairs. Ask and answer the questions from Exercise 6.

The best place to hang out

🎧 3.10

Teenagers just love shopping centres. In fact, research in the UK shows that teens make 40 per cent more trips to shopping centres than other age groups. Do they go there just for the shops? Are there other reasons? Our reporter Charlie Sandler finds out.

I visited the Northbourne Shopping Centre last weekend and interviewed some young teens.

Q When do you usually come here?
Laura I mainly come on Saturdays.
Archie I sometimes come on Sundays, too. But not during the week.

Q Who do you come here with?
Maria I come with my best friend, Laura!
Josh   I come here on my own or with my parents. But we don't stay together the whole time.

Q What do you do when you're here?
Archie We sit around and chat and look for our mates.
Laura We often have a smoothie and a muffin. It's a great place to chat.
Maria I love looking in all the different shops. But I don't buy much!

Q Why do you like this shopping centre?
Maria There are loads of shops and cafés. There are Chinese, Japanese and Mexican restaurants. And there's a multi-screen cinema, too.
Josh   It's warm and dry so it's a great place to hang out in the winter.

Q Who thinks the shopping centre is attractive?
Laura I do! I love the trees and all the bright lights.
Archie I love all the space. Lots of people come here but it never feels crowded.

Q Who likes the atmosphere?
Maria I think we all like it. It's friendly and relaxed.

Q How would you improve this shopping centre?
Josh   I'd change the music. It's a bit boring!
Laura I'd like to see more bright colours. There's too much white.

Q Which do you prefer – the shopping centre or the park?
Laura It depends on the weather. I think the shopping centre is my favourite place. But I prefer hanging out in the park in the summer.

Your Space   Talking about shopping

8 **Work in groups. Discuss the questions.**

- Is there a shopping centre where you live? What can you find there?
- Do you like shopping centres? Why? / Why not? How often do you go to them?
- Do you like shopping? Do you enjoy window shopping (you don't buy anything, you just look)?

® Question words

Get it right!

When using *did* in past simple questions, don't forget to keep the main verb in the present form.

What did you **watch** at the cinema?

NOT ~~What did you watched at the cinema?~~

1 **Complete the past simple questions with a question word from the box and the correct form of the verb.**

> what who where why when how

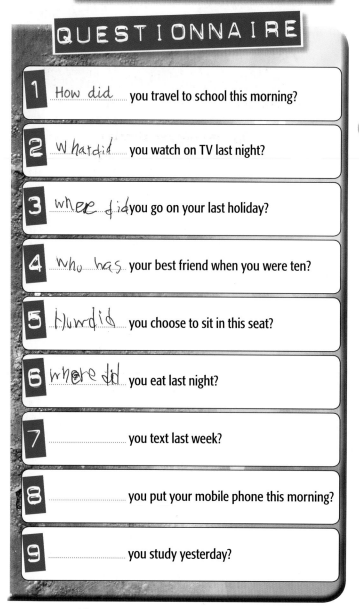

QUESTIONNAIRE

1 *How did* you travel to school this morning?

2 *What did* you watch on TV last night?

3 *where did* you go on your last holiday?

4 *Who has* your best friend when you were ten?

5 *How did* you choose to sit in this seat?

6 *where did* you eat last night?

7 .... you text last week?

8 .... you put your mobile phone this morning?

9 .... you study yesterday?

2 ☆ **Work in pairs. Ask and answer the questions. Make up new questions.**

Subject and object questions

- In this question, *who* refers to the object.

  OBJECT   SUBJECT

  (Who) does (this book) belong to?

  SUBJECT   OBJECT

  (This book) belongs to (Paul).

- In this question *who* refers to the subject.

  SUBJECT   OBJECT

  (Who) made (this cake)?

  SUBJECT   OBJECT

  (Paul) made (this cake).

3 **Write questions with the verbs below. You must know the answers to your questions.**

> wrote   invented   played   acted in
>
> won   sang   sailed   painted

1 Who .... ?
2 Who .... ?
3 Who .... ?
4 Who .... ?
5 Who .... ?
6 Who .... ?
7 Who .... ?
8 Who .... ?

Who wrote The Lord of the Rings?

4 ☆ **Work in groups. Ask and answer your questions. Who can get the most correct answers?**

A Who wrote *The Lord of the Rings*?
B I'm not sure. Did Shakespeare write it?
C No, he didn't. I think ...

5 Put the words in the correct order to make questions.

THE BIG QUIZ

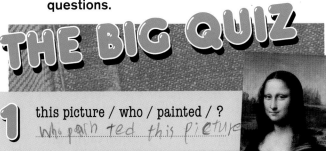

1 this picture / who / painted / ?
Who parn ted this picture

2 fly / did / how / the Montgolfier brothers / ?
How did the Montgolfier

3 did / what / Levi Strauss / invent / ?
What did Levi

4 Christopher Columbus / was / where / born / ?
where Christopher Columbus was?

5 which / won / the 2010 basketball World Championship / team / ?
_wh_

6 walk / did / Neil Armstrong / on the Moon / when / ?
when did Neil Armstrong

7 this building / who / built / ?
Who built this
_bi_

8 this character / created by / who / was / ?
who this character
created by

6 ☆ Work in pairs. Answer the questions.

7 🔘 **3.11** Listen and check your answers.

8 ✏ Work in groups. Write five more questions. You must know the answers.

9 ☆ Ask and answer your questions with another group. Who gets the most correct answers?

➡ **Language check page 132**

Use of *like*

like = enjoy things

I don't like cities.

be like = ask for a description

What's the weather like? It's stormy.

look like = say things are similar

Jake looks like his father!

would like = want something

Would you like a cake? Yes, I would.

10 **Answer these questions.**

1 What type of films do you like?
2 Would you like to visit New York?
3 Do you look like your father or your mother?
4 What type of music do you like?
5 What's your best friend like?
6 Do you like baseball?
7 What is your bedroom like?
8 What would you like to eat for dinner tonight?

Reading

1 **Warm up** What do you find in a modern city? Work in pairs. Brainstorm ideas. Think about:

tall buildings

(buildings)   (transport)   (shopping)   (entertainment)

museums

2 **Work in groups and compare your ideas. Then discuss these questions**

How many of these things were found in ancient cities? What was different about ancient cities?

3 **Read the article. Match the headings with the paragraphs.**

A Back to the past **B** Ancient cities **C** Megacities **D** Changing cities **E** Why cities developed

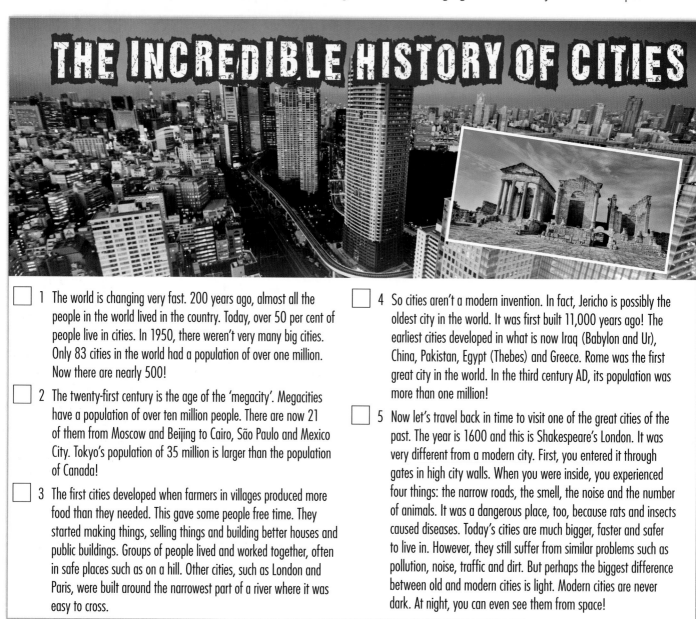

THE INCREDIBLE HISTORY OF CITIES

□ 1 The world is changing very fast. 200 years ago, almost all the people in the world lived in the country. Today, over 50 per cent of people live in cities. In 1950, there weren't very many big cities. Only 83 cities in the world had a population of over one million. Now there are nearly 500!

□ 2 The twenty-first century is the age of the 'megacity'. Megacities have a population of over ten million people. There are now 21 of them from Moscow and Beijing to Cairo, São Paulo and Mexico City. Tokyo's population of 35 million is larger than the population of Canada!

□ 3 The first cities developed when farmers in villages produced more food than they needed. This gave some people free time. They started making things, selling things and building better houses and public buildings. Groups of people lived and worked together, often in safe places such as on a hill. Other cities, such as London and Paris, were built around the narrowest part of a river where it was easy to cross.

□ 4 So cities aren't a modern invention. In fact, Jericho is possibly the oldest city in the world. It was first built 11,000 years ago! The earliest cities developed in what is now Iraq (Babylon and Ur), China, Pakistan, Egypt (Thebes) and Greece. Rome was the first great city in the world. In the third century AD, its population was more than one million!

□ 5 Now let's travel back in time to visit one of the great cities of the past. The year is 1600 and this is Shakespeare's London. It was very different from a modern city. First, you entered it through gates in high city walls. When you were inside, you experienced four things: the narrow roads, the smell, the noise and the number of animals. It was a dangerous place, too, because rats and insects caused diseases. Today's cities are much bigger, faster and safer to live in. However, they still suffer from similar problems such as pollution, noise, traffic and dirt. But perhaps the biggest difference between old and modern cities is light. Modern cities are never dark. At night, you can even see them from space!

4 Read the article again and answer the questions.

1 How many cities have a population of over one million?
2 How many people live in a megacity?
3 Where were the first cities built?
4 In which modern countries were the earliest cities?
5 How was Shakespeare's London different from a modern city?
6 How are old and modern cities similar?

5 Write three more questions about the article. Then ask and answer with your partner.

Listening and speaking

6 ◉ 3.13 Listen to Zoe and Daniel talk about their cities. Make notes in the table.

	Zoe	Daniel
city		
where it is		
population		
interesting to visit		
famous for		
problems		
best thing		

7 ◉ 3.13 Listen again. Who says these things Zoe (Z) or Daniel (D)?

1 Sometimes I don't like the weather. ☐
2 You can cycle everywhere and it's really safe. ☐
3 It's really great for kids and young people! ☐
4 At the weekend we go for walks on the waterfront. ☐
5 There are musicians, jugglers, magicians and clowns. ☐
6 It's got a lot of hills and we've got cable cars as well as buses. ☐
7 There are amazing parades and parties in the street. ☐
8 There are monkeys living up there! ☐

8 Work in pairs. Talk about a city in your country. Use the table in Exercise 6 to help you.

Writing

9 Write about a city in your country. Use your ideas from Exercise 8.

Study skills

Writing about a city
Copy and complete the table in Exercise 6. Make extra notes about the most important sights. Think of descriptive adjectives: *busy, beautiful, old, exciting,* etc. When you write your text, use linking words: *and, but, so, because,* etc. Start the last sentence: *But the best thing about/in my city is … because …*

10A I used to listen to rock and roll!

Grammar
used to / didn't use to

Functions
talking about your family

Vocabulary • Technology

1 🔘 **3.16 Match the words with the pictures. Then listen and check.**

a phone box ☐   a record ☐   a video ☐   a fountain pen ☐
a typewriter ☐   a cassette ☐   a black and white TV ☐   a camera ☐

2 Work in pairs. Ask and answer questions about the items in Exercise 1.

A Have you ever listened to a record?
B No, I haven't. But I know my grandparents have. And they still have an old record player. What about you?
A I listened to some records last summer!

Presentation

3 Warm up Quickly read the article on page 99. What objects from Exercise 1 does John mention?

4 🔘 **3.17 Listen and read the article again. Answer the questions.**

1 What type of music did John like?
2 How were his clothes different in the past?
3 Why was using a phone box boring?
4 What type of books did he read?
5 Why did he use his typewriter?
6 What did he want to become in the future?

5 Read *Language focus*. Then <u>underline</u> more examples of *used to* in the article.

6 Discuss the questions.

1 How did John listen to music in the past? How does he listen to music today?
2 How did he contact his friends in the past? What does he do today?

Language focus

- I **used to** buy all their records.
- We **didn't use to** have mobile phones.
- What **did you use to** do in your free time?

Then ... and now!

This week we're looking at the present and the past. And Holly has interviewed somebody very special ... her grandfather, John! How has his life changed since he was a teen? Read on and find out!

What kind of music did you listen to?
Well, I was a teenager in the 1960s so I used to listen to rock 'n' roll! I loved The Beatles and the Rolling Stones. I didn't use to have much money – but I bought all their records. And then in the 1970s I got into Pink Floyd and some rock bands like Led Zeppelin.

How did you use to listen to music?
I used to have a record player. We listened to albums and singles. I still have a lot of my old records but I never listen to them. But in the 1970s I used to buy cassettes. These days I listen to music on my mp3 player.

Were clothes important to you?
They still are important to me! But I used to wear very different clothes when I was a teen! I wore very colourful shirts and some of them had flowers on them! My trousers were a different size, too. But I still wear jeans, of course.

How did you use to contact your friends?
We didn't use to have mobile phones or computers then. We didn't even have a telephone in my house! I used to go to a phone box – with lots of coins! You had to wait if there were already people in the phone box. That was really boring, too. These days I never go anywhere without my mobile phone. I couldn't live without it!

What did you use to do in your free time?
I used to read loads of science fiction novels. And I used to write sci-fi stories on my old typewriter. They were terrible! I still read a lot, but I haven't read any sci-fi for years. I used to watch TV every day. But of course in the '60s it was black and white. And I used to listen to music with my friends and dream of being a rock star!

Your Space   Talking about your family

7   **Choose one of your grandparents and make notes.**

- Name
- Date of birth
- Place of birth
- Jobs
- Important events

8   **Work in pairs. Talk about your grandparents.**

A My grandmother was born in Athens in Greece.
B Really? When was she born?

used to / didn't use to

- We use *used to* to talk about our life in the past.

1 Write sentences about Jason. Use the verbs and the information below.

| be | have | wear | like |

Jason used to be a rock star. Now he's a bank clerk.

	1990	Today
Career	rock star	bank clerk
Appearance	dark hair	bald
Clothes	jeans and T-shirts	jacket, shirt and tie
Likes	skiing rock and heavy metal	golf country and western

2 Think of when you started your first school. How are you different now, and how are you the same? Write six sentences using *used to / didn't use to*.

| watch | play | wear | have | be |
| eat | drink | live | listen to | go |

I used to watch cartoons on TV.
I didn't use to eat much fruit.

3 ☆ Work in pairs. Talk about the changes in your life, and the things that have stayed the same.

A I used to watch cartoons on TV, and I still do!

B I didn't use to eat much fruit, but now I do.

4 Work in pairs. Look at the two pictures. How has Warnford changed in 50 years? Write as many sentences as possible.

Warnford 50 years ago

Warnford now

There used to be a bus stop.
There didn't use to be a car park.
There were lots of trees but now ...

 Get it right!

When you talk about routine in the present don't use *used to*.

I usually have coffee for breakfast.
NOT ~~I used to have coffee for breakfast.~~

used to – questions

5 Work in pairs. Read the role cards and act out the interview.

Student A

You are a journalist. Your partner is an astronaut. Ten years ago he/she spent a year on a space station. Ask questions.

What / do in your free time   What / eat
What / wear outside   What / wear inside
How / keep fit   Where / sleep

Student B

You are an astronaut. Ten years ago you spent a year on a space station. Think about:

your routine   your free time   your clothes
your food   your likes and dislikes

Answer the journalist's questions.

A What did you use to do in your free time?
B I used to read and write a diary.

6 Read the role cards and act out the interview.

Student A

You are a scientist. Five years ago you spent a year on an Antarctic Research Station. Think about:

your routine   your free time   your clothes
your food   your likes and dislikes

Answer the journalist's questions.

Student B

You are a journalist. Your partner is a scientist. Five years ago he/she spent a year on an Antarctic Research Station. Ask questions.

What / do every day   What / wear outside
What / wear inside   How / keep fit
Where / sleep   What / listen to

7 Compare your life with the lives of your grandparents. Think about the following topics.

technology   contacting friends

food and drink   music

transport   free time

My grandparents used to buy records and cassettes. I download my music.

8 Work in groups. Compare your ideas from Exercise 7.

Soundbite

/p/ /b/

A 3.18 Listen and circle the words you hear.

	A	B
1	pear	bear
2	pin	bin
3	pen	Ben
4	Paul	ball
5	pie	buy
6	cap	cab
7	peach	beach
8	pig	big

B Work in pairs. Take turns to say a word from Exercise A. Your partner says if it is an 'A' or 'B' word.

C 3.19 Listen and repeat the tongue-twisters.

1 I put my book in my bag and my passport in my pocket.
2 The pool wasn't big so we played ball on the beach.

Grammar
general language review ®

Functions
fluency practice

Vocabulary • Review

1 Work in pairs. Copy the spidergrams and add your ideas.

cousin

free time   family   films   jobs

fire fighter

skateboarding   actor

2 Work in pairs. Choose one of the topics from Exercise 1 and try to keep a conversation going for two minutes. Ask and answer questions.

A I'd like to be a vet.
B Why do you want to do that?
A You can work with lots of different animals.
B What are your favourite animals?
A Horses. I love them! What about you?

3 Choose another topic and try it again.

Presentation

4 Work in groups. Read the rules for the board game. Then start talking!

Talk about it!

Play the game in groups of three: A, B and C

- You need a coin and counters.
- If you throw heads, move one square.
- If you throw tails, move two squares.
- The first player tosses the coin and answers the question. The group can ask more questions. Try to talk for one minute!
- The winner is the first person to reach the end.

END *You're the winner!*

What will you do if it's sunny on Saturday?

Talk about somebody you admire.

Where would you go if you could travel in time?

MISS A TURN!

Do you download anything?

What have you already done today?

What would you do if you won a lot of money?

Do you ever visit websites in English?

Have you ever been to another country?

What are you going to do later today?

MISS A TURN!

Look at your clothes. Where were they made?

FREE QUESTION! Another player asks you a question.

What are your school rules?

Talk about the last book you read.

What chores do you have to do at home?

FREE QUESTION! Another player asks you a question.

What did you use to do when you were five?

What were you doing at 6 pm on Sunday?

A

B

START

C

Talk about somewhere you like.

END *You're the winner!*

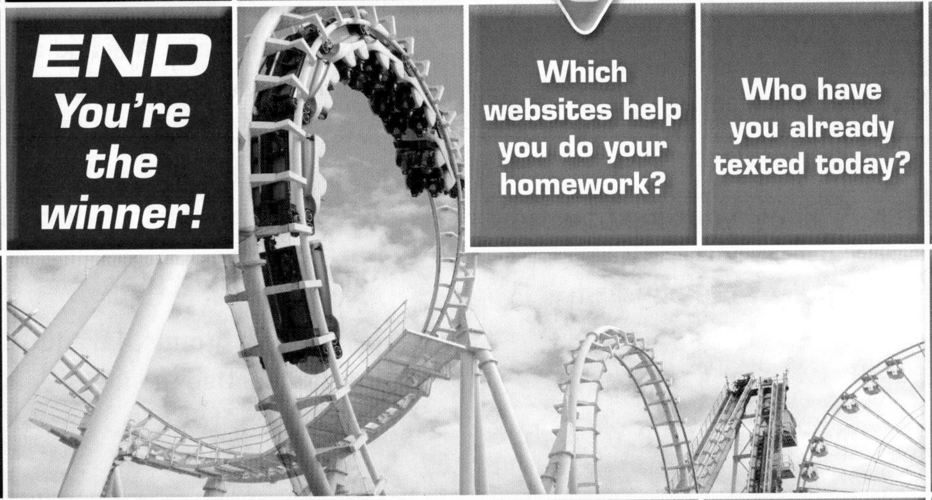

Which websites help you do your homework?

Who have you already texted today?

What do you have too much / not enough of?

END *You're the winner!*

Talk about something you always carry with you.

Have you ever written a diary or a blog?

MISS A TURN!

You can't sleep at night. Ask for advice!

What would you do if you had more free time?

What are you going to do at the weekend?

FREE QUESTION! Another player asks you a question.

Ⓡ Present perfect

1 Harry is getting ready for his holiday. Write sentences with *already* and *yet*.

He hasn't packed his cap yet.

pack cap	turn off computer
buy a guide book	tidy room
make bed	find passport
print out bus ticket	

Where's my passport?

Ⓡ Present perfect and past simple

2 🗨 Work in pairs. Change roles after three minutes.

Student A

Ask questions with *How long* and the ideas below. Then ask more questions using the past simple.

Student B

Use *for* and *since* in your first answer. Then answer all of your partner's questions.

use a computer   know your best friend

live in your home   study English

live in this town   be at this school

know me   have your favourite T-shirt

A How long have you known your best friend?
B I've known my best friend for three years.
A When did you meet?
B We met in the school holidays.
A Where did you meet?

First conditional

3 🖊 Complete the sentences for you.

What if ...?

Hi! Today's blog asks you to think about the next few days.

If I go to bed very late tonight,
....

If it's cold and wet tomorrow,
....

If I don't do my homework,
....

If I don't eat my dinner this evening,
....

If I spend my pocket money,
....

If I talk in class,
....

If I don't remember my school bag,
....

4 🗨 Work in pairs. Ask and answer questions about the sentences in Exercise 3.

A What will happen if you go to bed very late tonight?
B I won't wake up in the morning!

Second conditional

5 🗨 Work in groups. Take turns to continue the stories. Use the ideas below.

If I went to Australia, ...   If I were a film star, ...

If I had a time travel machine, ...   If I were 65, ...

A If I went to Australia, I'd visit the Great Barrier Reef.
B If I visited the Great Barrier Reef, I'd go swimming.
C If I went swimming, ...

Reported speech

6 Work in pairs. Read the rules. Then play the game.

> Take turns to report what the people said.
>
> You get two points for each correct answer.
>
> If your partner thinks you are wrong, check with your teacher.

A David is learning the guitar.
B He said (that) David was learning the guitar.

Student A
- David is learning the guitar.
- Lisa can't speak Russian.
- You have to walk the dog.
- You mustn't play your music too loud.
- I can't find my mobile phone.
- Are you thinking about your holiday?

Student B
- I hate getting up early in the morning.
- Is there anything to eat?
- My parents don't like heavy metal.
- Nick won't reply to my phone calls.
- Is Harry coming to my party?
- I send 50 text messages every day.

Language check page 132

Your words 10B

Multi-word verbs

Multi-word verbs combine prepositions with common verbs. Here are some useful ones.

find out

I've found out all about volcanoes on the internet.

go back

I had to go back to school because I forgot my bag.

look for

Where's my mobile phone? I've looked for it everywhere!

look after

My friend looks after my cat when I'm on holiday.

put away

Put away all your things! It's time for dinner.

make up

... and then I saw a tiger!
My little sister makes up incredible stories!

7 Match the verbs with the prepositions to make more multi-word verbs. Then write a sentence for each one.

hang	take	sit	put	turn	give

up	out	down	away	on	off

hang out: I like hanging out with my friends.

Reading

1 **Warm up** Imagine you are a world-famous sports star and discuss the questions.

What are the good things about your life? What are the bad things? How has your life changed?

2 **Read the article about Carlos Acosta quickly. Does it mention any of your ideas?**

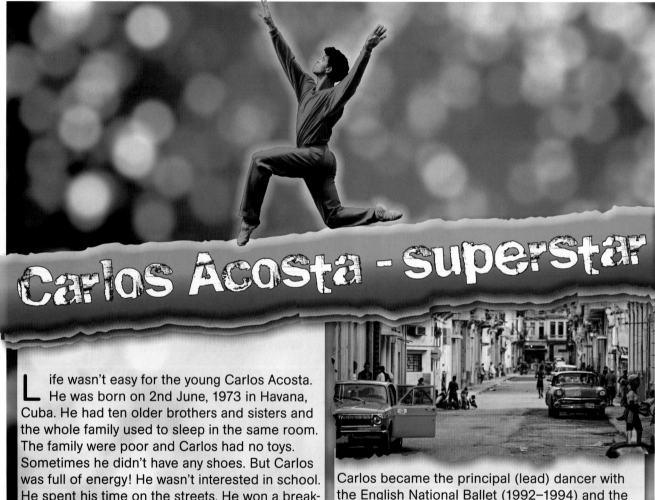

Carlos Acosta - superstar

Life wasn't easy for the young Carlos Acosta. He was born on 2nd June, 1973 in Havana, Cuba. He had ten older brothers and sisters and the whole family used to sleep in the same room. The family were poor and Carlos had no toys. Sometimes he didn't have any shoes. But Carlos was full of energy! He wasn't interested in school. He spent his time on the streets. He won a break-dancing competition when he was only nine! His dream was to be a professional footballer. However, his father had a different idea. In 1980, he sent Carlos to a dance school. He had two reasons for this – dance schools offered a free lunch every day, and they taught discipline.

So Carlos started going to the National Ballet School of Cuba ... and he hated it. He found the physical exercises boring and he wanted to hang out with his friends. But when he was 13, he saw his first real ballet – and he knew that he wanted to become a great dancer. 'I found that ballet was my best friend,' he said. 'I was determined to be the best I could.' He won his first important dance prize in 1990 when he was only 16.

Carlos became the principal (lead) dancer with the English National Ballet (1992–1994) and the Houston Ballet (1993–1998). He has danced with all the world's great dance companies including the Bolshoi and the Royal Ballet. In 2003 he wrote, choreographed and danced in *Tocororo (A Cuban Tale)*. This show is about a young boy who leaves his home in the countryside for a new life in the city. It was similar to his own experiences.

Carlos Acosta is a successful and brilliant artist. He is loved by audiences all over the world. Yet in his autobiography *No Way Home* (published in 2007), he talked about the tough, lonely and painful world of ballet. He also wrote about his sadness at living away from Cuba. But he loves dancing. And every time he dances, he is happy.

3 **Read the article again and number the events in the correct order.**

- ☐ He performed in his own ballet, *Tocororo*, in 2003.
- ☐ 10 His autobiography, *No Way Home*, was published.
- ☐ He won an important dance competition when he was 16.
- ☐ He disliked the National Ballet School.
- ☐ He wanted to become a footballer.
- ☐ He joined the English National Ballet.
- ☐ He was sent to dance school in 1980.
- ☐ He won a break-dancing competition when he was nine.
- ☐ 1 Carlos was born to a poor family in Havana.
- ☐ He danced with the Houston Ballet.

4 **Work in groups. Discuss the questions.**

What do you think Carlos learned at dance school? How did it change his life?
Why does he sometimes feel lonely and sad?

Study skills

Putting events in order
Read the article two or three times. Draw a timeline and write the main events on it. Use dates, ages and words like *Then*. Use a pencil to order the events. Read the article again to check your facts.

Listening and speaking

5 ◎ 3.21 **Listen and match the people and the information. Write *T* (Theresa) or *D* (David).**

- Montreal ☐
- a tree house ☐
- San Diego ☐
- a bunch of flowers ☐
- an apartment ☐
- wet hair ☐
- a teddy bear ☐
- a water pistol ☐

6 ◎ 3.21 **Work in pairs. Try to remember the questions. Then listen again and check.**

7 **Write four true facts and invent one false piece of information about your life.**

I was born in ...
The first house I lived in was ...
When I was little I used to ...

8 **Tell the class your facts. Answer any questions. The class has to discover the false information.**

Writing

9 **Think about a grown-up that you know. Make notes:**

- **Appearance and personality**
  What do they look like? What are they like? What do they do?
- **Birth and childhood**
  Where and when were they born? Who were their parents? Where was their first home?
- **Education and teen years**
  Where did they study? What subjects were they good at? What were their interests? What did they do in their free time?

10 **Write the beginning of a short biography. Use your notes to write three paragraphs.**

1 Communication

Asking about rules

1 Look at the Meadow Sports Centre rules. Then match the questions with the answers.

Alice asks …

1 Is it OK to chew gum? `d`
2 Are you allowed to take photos? ☐
3 Do I have to shower before swimming? ☐
4 Can I use the weights room? ☐
5 Is it OK to drink water in the gym area? ☐
6 Are you allowed to come here with friends? ☐

Adam answers …

a Sure. No problem.
b Yes, you are. You can bring one guest with you.
c No, it's not allowed. And you must leave your mobile in your locker, too.
d No, I'm sorry, you can't.
e Yes, you do.
f No, I'm sorry. You have to be over 16.

Meadow Sports Centre

RULES

- Wear appropriate sports clothes and shoes.
- No chewing gum.
- No food or drink in the gym area except water.
- No under-16s in the weights room.
- Look after your belongings.
- No mobile phones or cameras.
- Shower before you go in the swimming pool.
- You can bring a guest once a week.

2 ◉ 1.10 Listen and check. Then act out the conversations.

3 ◉ 1.11 Look at *Phrasebook*. Listen and repeat.

4 Work in pairs. Role play a conversation.

Student A You are at a sports club. Ask the receptionist about the rules.

Student B You are the receptionist at the gym. Answer Student A's questions.

Begin:
A Can I ask you about some of the rules?
B Yes, of course …

Finish:
A OK, thanks very much for your help.

Phrasebook

Asking about rules
Can I … ?
Are you allowed to … ?
Is it OK to … ?
Do I have to … ?

Replying
Sure. No problem.
Of course you can.
No, I'm sorry, you can't.
No, it's not allowed.

Describing a picture

1 **Warm up** **Work in pairs. Look at the photos and answer the questions.**

What can you see in the photos? Where are the people? What are they doing?
Can you identify the city? Would you like to visit it?

2 **1.20** **Listen to the conversation and decide which photo the people are talking about.**

3 **1.21** **Look at *Phrasebook*. Listen and repeat.**

4 **Work in pairs. Choose one of the other photos from Exercise 1 and describe it to your partner. Remember to ask questions.**

5 **Work in pairs and follow the instructions.**

> **Student A**
> Choose a picture in the book. Don't show your partner!
> Then describe it. Answer any questions.

> **Student B**
> Listen to your partner's description of the picture and ask questions. Then try to find the picture in the book.

6 **Swap roles and repeat Exercise 5.**

> **Phrasebook**
>
> **Describing a picture**
> In the foreground ...
> I can see ...
> In the centre ...
> In the background ...
> On the right ...
> On the left ...
> She looks ...
> I think she's ...
> **Asking for more details**
> Can you describe it?
> What else can you see?
> What does she look like?
> What's she doing?

Negotiating

1   Read and follow the instructions.

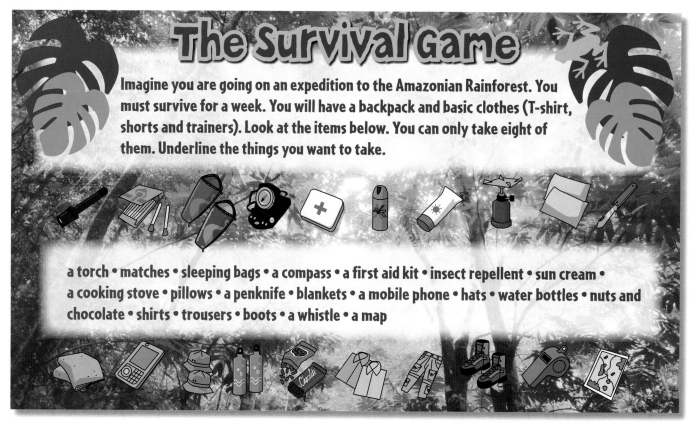

The Survival Game

Imagine you are going on an expedition to the Amazonian Rainforest. You must survive for a week. You will have a backpack and basic clothes (T-shirt, shorts and trainers). Look at the items below. You can only take eight of them. Underline the things you want to take.

a torch • matches • sleeping bags • a compass • a first aid kit • insect repellent • sun cream • a cooking stove • pillows • a penknife • blankets • a mobile phone • hats • water bottles • nuts and chocolate • shirts • trousers • boots • a whistle • a map

2   ⊙ 1.31 Listen and complete the conversation.

let's   good   going   decided   don't   ~~think~~   should

Amy	Shall we take blankets? It can be cold at night.
Max	Erm ... I'm not sure. What do you ¹ _think_ ?
Ella	I ² _____ agree. We ³ _____ take sleeping bags. They're lighter than blankets, too.
Max	I think Ella's right. Sleeping bags are better.
Amy	OK, so we're ⁴ _____ to take sleeping bags. What else?
Max	⁵ _____ take insect repellent.
Amy	That's a ⁶ _____ idea.
Ella	I agree. Insects will be a big problem.
Amy	Great! So we've ⁷ _____ to take insect repellent, too.

3   ⊙ 1.32 Look at *Phrasebook*. Listen and repeat. Copy the intonation.

4   Work in groups. Decide which eight items you are going to take. Then compare your choices with the rest of the class.

Phrasebook

Suggesting
Let's take …
We should take …
Shall we take … ?

Checking
Why do you want to take … ?
What do you think?

Being unsure
I'm not sure.

Agreeing and disagreeing
I agree. / I don't agree.
That's a good idea.

Rounding up
So, we're going to take …
So, we've decided to take …

4 | Communication

Buying clothes

1 Warm up Work in pairs. Discuss the questions.

How often do you go shopping for clothes? What clothes have you bought recently?
Where do you normally buy your clothes? Do you enjoy shopping for clothes?

2 ⊙ 1.39 Read and put the conversation in order. Then listen and check.

1	**Sales assistant**	Can I help you?
2	**Francesco**	Yes, please. I'm looking for a sweater. Have you got one in blue?
☐	**Sales assistant**	Yes, no problem. Is that any better?
☐	**Sales assistant**	Here you are.
3	**Sales assistant**	What size are you?
☐	**Sales assistant**	Yes, of course. How does it feel?
☐	**Francesco**	Yes, thanks. How much is it?
☐	**Francesco**	I'm a medium, I think.
☐	**Francesco**	Can I try it on?
☐	**Francesco**	It's a bit small. Could I try on a larger one?
11	**Sales assistant**	£20.
12	**Francesco**	I'll take this one, please.

3 ⊙ 1.40 Look at *Phrasebook*. Listen and complete. Then listen and repeat.

4 Work in pairs. Act out the conversation from Exercise 2.

5 ⊙ 1.41 Listen to some more conversations and complete the table.

	What do they want?	What size do they take?	How much do the items cost?
I Erin			
2 Lewis			
3 Amelia			

6 Choose from the items below and act out more conversations.

Phrasebook

Can I help you?
I'm just ¹................ , thanks.
I'm ²................ some jeans.
Have you got them ³................ black?
What size are you? / What size do you take?
I'm a ⁴................ . / I'm a size 38.
⁵................ I ⁶................ them on?
They're a ⁷................ small.
Have you got a ⁸................ pair?
How much are they?
I'll ⁹................ them.

➡ **WB page 33** | Communication   **Unit 4 111**

Going to the doctor's

1 Warm up **Work in pairs. Look at the picture and discuss the questions.**

What do you think is wrong with the patient?
When did you last go to the doctor's?

2 🔊 **2.10** **Work in pairs. Listen and complete the conversations with the words in the box. Then role play the situations.**

> temperature   prescription   cough   examine   ~~matter~~   accident   hospital   hurt   pain

A Doctor Hello, please sit down. Now, what's the ¹ _matter_ ?
Keira I've got a terrible sore throat and a ² _____ .
I've had it for a week now.
Doctor Have you got a ³ _____ ?
Keira Yes, I have. It's about 38.
Doctor Let me ⁴ _____ you. Mmm, take a deep breath in … and out. Open your mouth. Well, you've got an infection. Here's a ⁵ _____ for some antibiotics. Take one three times a day after meals. And don't go to school this week.
Keira Thanks, doctor. Goodbye.

B Doctor Hello. How are you today?
Marek Not great! I've got a terrible ⁶ _____ in my ankle.
Doctor Oh dear. Take off your shoe so I can examine it. Does that ⁷ _____ ?
Marek Ouch! Yes, it does.
Doctor Did you have an ⁸ _____ ?
Marek I hurt it in a football match two days ago.
Doctor Well, I think I'm going to send you to ⁹ _____ for an X-ray.

3 🔊 **2.11** **Listen and complete the notes.**

	Harvey	Gracie
Problem	feels _____ bad _____	gets _____ about _____ times a week
Doctor's advice	go _____ don't _____ but drink lots of water don't go _____	get some _____ do something _____

4 🔊 **2.12** **Look at *Phrasebook*. Listen and repeat. Copy the intonation.**

5 **Work in pairs. Take turns to role play conversations at the doctor's.**

Phrasebook

Doctor
What's the matter?
What seems to be the problem?
Have you got a headache?
Let me examine you.
Here's a prescription.
Patient
I've got a sore throat.
I've got a pain in my ankle.
I feel really ill.
Thank you, doctor.

Taking messages

1 **Warm up** **Look at the pictures and answer the questions.**

What do you think is happening? What do you think they are talking about?

2 🔘 **2.25** **Listen to the conversation and correct the message.**

3 🔘 **2.25** **Listen again and complete the conversation.**

Can I take I'll give Where did you say ~~Could I speak~~ what did you say

Nicole	Hello.
Tyler	Hello. ¹ _Could I speak_ to Lexi, please?
Nicole	I'm sorry, she isn't here. ² _____ a message?
Tyler	Yes, please. Could you tell her Tyler called?
Nicole	Sorry, ³ _____ ?
Tyler	Could you tell her Tyler called? Can she meet me outside the Pegasus cinema?
Nicole	⁴ _____ , exactly?
Tyler	The Pegasus cinema. At quarter past two. The film starts at half past.
Nicole	OK. Has she got your number?
Tyler	Yes, I think so. But I'll give it again. It's 0769 57438840.
Nicole	OK, ⁵ _____ Lexi the message. Bye.
Tyler	Thanks, bye.

Lexi
Tyler called
meet at cinema at 3.15
film starts at 3.30
please call him
mobile no.
0769 57348840

4 🔘 **2.26** **Listen and complete the messages.**

1
.... called
call before ....
needs help with ....
number ....

2
.... called
meet .... in park
at ....
take ....

5 🔘 **2.27** **Look at *Phrasebook*. Listen and repeat.**

6 **Work in pairs. Role play your own conversations. Take turns to leave and take messages. Before you begin, make notes:**

• decide who you are • decide who the message is for • invent your message

Phrasebook

Leaving a message
Could I leave a message?
Can you tell her Amy called?

Taking a message
Can I take a message?
Pardon?
Sorry, what did you say?
Where did you say?
Could you repeat that, please?
Can you spell that, please?
OK, I'll give her the message.

Giving advice

1   **⊙ 2.36 Work in pairs. Listen and complete the conversations. Then act them out.**

| really | sure | but | should | ~~problem~~ | maybe | you | why |

A **Zara**   Hey, what's up?
   Leo   I'm really worried about my exams.
   Zara   What's the ¹ _problem_ ?
   Leo   I've done a lot of work, but I'm so nervous I can't sleep at night.
   Zara   ² _____ don't you read a book or a magazine when you go to bed?
   Leo   I'm not ³ _____ that's a good idea. The trouble is I can't stop thinking about the exam!
   Zara   If I were ⁴ _____ , I'd do some exercise. That'll help you relax.
   Leo   Thanks, I'll try that.

B **Billy**   Are you OK?
   Lauren   Not ⁵ _____ . I'm bored because I haven't got enough money to do anything.
   Billy   ⁶ _____ you could ask your parents for some money.
   Lauren   Yes, ⁷ _____ I've asked them too many times.
   Billy   I see. I think you ⁸ _____ learn to do inline skating. You can use my old skates. You don't need money for that!
   Lauren   That's a good idea! Thanks!

2   **⊙ 2.37 Look at *Phrasebook*. Listen and repeat. Copy the intonation.**

3   **Choose one of the problems below. Think about how you feel, why the situation is difficult, etc. Make notes.**

   I've borrowed my friend's scarf and now I've lost it.
   I can't get up in the morning.
   I eat too much junk food.
   My six-year-old sister keeps taking my things.

4   **Work in pairs. Take turns to ask for advice.**

   Student A   **Student B**

   Ask if your friend is OK.
                                     Explain your problem.

   Offer some advice.
                                     Express doubt and give a reason.

   Offer different advice.
                                     Accept the advice and say thank you.

Phrasebook

Giving advice
If I were you, …
Why don't you … ?
I think you should …
Maybe you could …

Expressing doubt
I'm not sure that's a good idea.
The trouble is …
Yes, but …

Accepting advice
That's a good idea.
Thanks. I'll try that.

Talking about feelings

1 **Warm up Work in pairs. Discuss the questions.**

How do you feel today? How did you feel yesterday?
What makes you feel happy / sad / nervous / excited?

2 **3.04 Listen and number the pictures.**

3 **3.04 Listen again and complete the conversations. Choose from the adjectives in the box.**

nervous(x2) happy sad depressed bored upset excited scared worried embarrassed

1 **Eric**   Hi there.
   Sophie   Oh, hello.
   Eric   What's wrong? You sound a bit
      ¹........................ .
   Sophie   Yeah, I feel really ² .... today.
   Eric   Why?
   Sophie   Because I've just heard my exam results.
      They weren't very good.
   Eric   Oh dear! I'm really sorry.

2 **Paul**   Are you alright? You look ³ ....
   Keira   I feel really ⁴ ....
   Paul   Why do you feel ⁵ .... ?
   Keira   Because I have to see the headmaster in
      ten minutes.
   Paul   What did you do?
   Keira   I was playing football when I kicked the ball
      through his window!
   Paul   Oh no!

3 **Tom**   Hi, Olivia.
   Olivia   Hi. You look ⁶ ....
   Tom   I am!
   Olivia   What's happened?
   Tom   I've just got a text from my dad.
      We're going to the USA in the
      summer! I'm so ⁷ .... !
   Olivia   That's great!

Phrasebook

Asking about feelings
Are you alright?
What's wrong?
What's up?
You look happy.
You don't look very well.
Talking about feelings
I'm so happy.
I feel nervous.
Giving reasons
I have to go to the dentist's.
Because I've just heard my
   exam results.

4 **3.05 Look at *Phrasebook*. Listen and repeat. Copy the intonation.**

5 **Act out the conversations. Sound worried, happy, etc.**

6 **Work in pairs. Choose a feeling from Exercise 3. Then make
conversations. Remember to give an explanation.**

Giving directions

Weston Shopping Centre

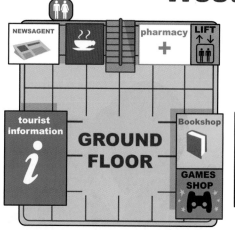
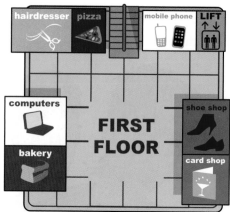

1 ⊙ **3.14** Listen and complete the conversations.

| stairs | lift | exactly | can't | ~~here~~ | tell | straight | much |

A Jack Excuse me. Is there a sports shop
¹ _____here_____ ?

Alice Yes, there is. Take the ² _____ to the
second floor. Then turn left and go ³ _____
on. It's on the left, next to the restaurant.

Jack So it's on the second floor on the left?

Alice That's right.

Jack Thanks very ⁴ _____ .

Alice No problem.

B Rachel Excuse me. Can you ⁵ _____ me where
the toilets are, please?

Juan Yes, they're on the ground floor.

Rachel Where ⁶ _____ ?

Juan Go down the ⁷ _____ and turn right.
There's a corridor between the café and
the newsagent's. Go along the corridor and
the toilets are at the end. You ⁸ _____
miss them.

Rachel Thank you.

Juan Not at all.

Phrasebook

Asking for directions

Excuse me. Is there a sports shop
here?

Where is the shoe shop?

Can you tell me where the
pharmacy is, please?

Giving directions

Go up the stairs to the first floor.

Take the lift to the second floor.

Go down to the ground floor.

Turn left. Go straight on.

Go along the corridor. It's next to
the café.

You can't miss it.

2 ⊙ **3.15** Look at *Phrasebook*. Listen and repeat.

3 Work in pairs. Start from different places in the shopping centre. Then choose other places
and ask for directions.

Saying goodbye

1 **3.22** Warm up **Listen to the conversations and match them with the situations.**

going away for a long time ☐   going home ☐   going on holiday ☐

2 **3.22** **Listen again and complete the conversations. Then act them out in groups.**

A	**Stefan**	It's getting ¹ _late_ . It's time for me to go.
	Luke	OK. See you, Stefan.
	Stefan	Yeah, bye. ² _____ you tomorrow.
	Mrs Hill	Bye, Stefan. See you soon.
	Stefan	Goodbye, Mrs Hill. ³ _____ seeing you.

B	**Chloe**	I'm going now. I have to pack!
	Sofia	Have a ⁴ _____ time.
	Chloe	I will, don't worry!
	Sofia	And ⁵ _____ me a postcard.
	Chloe	OK. I'll see you when I get back.

C	**Hailey**	We're leaving in the morning, so I've ⁶ _____ to say goodbye.
	Mrs Keaton	Oh, that's nice of you, Hailey. We're going to miss you.
	Hailey	I'm going to ⁷ _____ you, too.
	Nick	Now remember, ⁸ _____ in touch!
	Hailey	I will. ⁹ _____ me ... or we can chat online.
	Nick	And send me photos and everything.
	Mrs Keaton	¹⁰ _____ care. Have a good journey.
	Hailey	Thanks. Goodbye!

3 **3.23** **Look at** *Phrasebook*. **Listen and repeat. Copy the intonation.**

4 **Work in pairs. Write conversations for these situations. Use expressions from** *Phrasebook*. **Then act them out.**

> You are at a friend's house. A DVD has just finished. You decide to go home.

> You are going to live for a year in New York. You and your parents are leaving at the weekend.

Phrasebook

Saying goodbye
Leaving
It's time for me to go.
I'm afraid I have to go.
I'm going now.
I've come to say goodbye.
Goodbyes
Bye!/Goodbye.
See you!
See you tomorrow/soon.
Nice seeing you.
Take care!
Have a safe journey.
I'm going to miss you.
Call me. / Text me.
Keep in touch!

Irregular verbs

Verb	Past simple	Past participle
be	was/were	been
beat	beat	beaten
become	became	become
begin	began	begun
bite	bit	bitten
break	broke	broken
bring	brought	brought
build	built	built
buy	bought	bought
catch	caught	caught
choose	chose	chosen
come	came	come
cost	cost	cost
cut	cut	cut
do	did	done
drink	drank	drunk
drive	drove	driven
eat	ate	eaten
fall	fell	fallen
feel	felt	felt
fight	fought	fought
find	found	found
fly	flew	flown
forget	forgot	forgotten
get	got	got
give	gave	given
go	went	gone
grow	grew	grown
hang	hung	hung
have	had	had
hear	heard	heard
hit	hit	hit
hold	held	held
keep	kept	kept
know	knew	known

Verb	Past simple	Past participle
leave	left	left
lose	lost	lost
make	made	made
meet	met	met
pay	paid	paid
put	put	put
read	read	read
ride	rode	ridden
ring	rang	rung
run	ran	run
say	said	said
see	saw	seen
sell	sold	sold
send	sent	sent
shake	shook	shaken
sing	sang	sung
sink	sank	sunk
sit	sat	sat
sleep	slept	slept
speak	spoke	spoken
spend	spent	spent
stand	stood	stood
steal	stole	stolen
swim	swam	swum
take	took	taken
teach	taught	taught
tell	told	told
think	thought	thought
understand	understood	understood
upset	upset	upset
wake	woke	woken
wear	wore	worn
win	won	won
write	wrote	written

On the Dark Side of the Moon

by Martyn Hobbs

Contents

Episode 1 ● 3.24

A 500-metre-long vehicle moved silently against the blackness of space. The spaceship looked old and grey and dirty. There were no people on it, only robots. And their destination was the dark side of the Moon.

A tall girl with long red hair was watching the spaceship through a large window. From this position, she couldn't see the Earth or the Sun. But she could see the dark and mysterious Moon. Every day spaceships, called Rubbish Transporters, carried rubbish and dangerous materials from the Earth. And on the Moon, a Lunar Recycling Plant received all the rubbish and buried it or recycled it.

Nina was the only person interested in these Rubbish Transporters. This was her third day on space station *Alastor* and everything was new to her! Her parents were scientists and they had to work on the *Alastor* for a year. After 14 years on Earth, Nina's new life was very strange. In fact, she wasn't sure she liked living in space. She didn't miss the pollution and the noise on Earth, but she missed her friends. She felt sad when she thought about them ... about Clara and Isla and Aimee ... But then she heard voices behind her. She quickly wiped her eyes and turned.

The Alastor

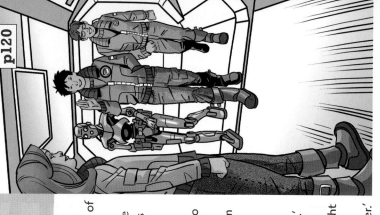

Two boys and a robot were walking along the corridor. The boys were laughing but the robot was talking seriously. One of the boys called out, 'Hey, Nina!'

It was Kai. He was in her class in the space station school. He was very funny and had a big smile. His best friend, Billy, was with him. Billy's nickname was 'Brains'.

'You have to do your homework,' said the robot.

'Oh come on, Charles. That's not fair,' said Kai. 'You don't do any homework.'

'I don't have time for any other work,' the robot replied. 'I'm always busy. I have to look after you.'

Kai smiled. 'OK, Charles. We're going to do our homework now. I promise. Are you happy?'

'I'm a robot, Kai,' said Charles. 'I'm never happy or unhappy.'

Of course, Kai knew Charles was a robot and robots didn't have emotions. But sometimes ... well, sometimes Kai thought Charles had a sense of humour.

'I must leave you now,' said Charles. 'I have to prepare dinner.'

They watched Charles walk away.

'Are we really going to do our homework?' asked Billy.

'Are you joking?' said Kai. 'I've got a better idea. Hey, Nina, do you want to come with us? We can show you a really cool place.'

Nina didn't have to do any homework. She always did her homework immediately after school. And she was pleased to be with her new friends.

Episode 2 🔘 3.25

Music from the past

Nina, Kai and Billy were walking along a bright white corridor. Kai wanted to hear about life on Earth. His family came to the *Alastor* over two years ago. He felt a bit homesick. Nina was talking about her old school and friends when Billy said, 'Wait a minute. Take a look in here, Nina.'

They were outside the Control Room. Through the glass window Nina could see about 15 adults and 30 robots. Some of them were studying computer screens. Some were talking into small microphones. Others were checking the routes of space traffic on a 3D map in the centre of the room. This room controlled the movements of the Rubbish Transporters from Earth.

'Can you see those people over there?' asked Kai. 'They're looking for Space Pirates.'

'Who are they?' asked Nina.

'They're criminal gangs that attack space vehicles,' said Billy.

'I hope they don't attack us!' said Nina, and they laughed.

'Do your parents know about this room?' asked Nina.

'No way!' Kai said.

'When did you find it?'

'I didn't find it,' said Kai. 'Billy did.'

'How did you find it?' Nina asked him.

'I was looking at a plan of the *Alastor*, for a school project,' Billy said, 'and I realised there was a space behind this wall.'

'Billy's very clever,' said Kai.

They walked on for about another 30 metres. Then they turned into an empty corridor. Billy took a small, red screwdriver from his pocket and pointed it at the wall. The screwdriver made a noise ... then Billy removed a plastic panel from the wall. Nina looked through the hole and saw a dark room. Billy turned on the light.

'After you, Nina,' said Billy politely. And Nina went in.

Nina looked around. There were pictures, lots of cushions, musical instruments and games. Then Nina pointed at a weird object next to Kai.

'What's that old thing?' she asked.

'It's ... er ... an mp3 player,' said Kai. Nina didn't understand. 'You can listen to music with it. This one was my great-grandad's. I'm going to play you his favourite music. It's so funny!'

So they listened to some really old songs. Kai played Madonna, Michael Jackson, Lady Gaga ... Nina didn't like any of the songs, but she didn't tell Kai and Billy. She didn't want to hurt their feelings. After about 20 minutes, her eyes felt very heavy.

She wasn't bored – she just couldn't stay awake! She looked at Billy and Kai. Billy was sleeping on the floor. Kai looked ill and he was holding his head. What was happening? Nina tried to stand up but she was too tired to move. Then a terrible darkness filled her mind. It was like the blackness of space. And she fell asleep ...

STORY On the Dark Side of the Moon

Episode 3 ○ 3.26

Alone

Nina woke up in the dark. She felt terrible. Her arms and legs were heavy, her mouth was dry, and her head was aching. She felt scared. Where was she? What was happening? Was she lost in space? Was she dead? Then she heard voices. Boys' voices. And she slowly remembered …

'Kai?' she whispered.

A voice came to her from out of the darkness.

'I'm over here,' Kai said. Nina looked but she couldn't see him.

'What happened?'

'I don't know. But I think we've been asleep for hours!'

Nina heard some banging noises.

'What's happening?' she asked.

'Don't worry, it's me,' said Billy. 'I'm trying … to find … the plastic panel … Yes!'

Billy pushed the panel into the corridor. Green light entered their secret room.

'Why are the lights green?' asked Nina.

'They're emergency lights,' said Billy, climbing out into the corridor.

'Then there isn't just a problem in here,' said Nina. 'There's a problem on the *Alastor*!'

She joined Billy and Kai in the corridor.

'Has this ever happened before?' she asked.

'No,' said Billy. Then they stood still and listened. They couldn't hear anything. The space station was silent.

'Come on,' said Kai. 'Let's find out what happened.'

They walked all over the *Alastor*. They explored the Control Room, the school, the restaurants, the cabins, the engine room. They walked along every corridor, they checked every room … and they didn't find another human being. Or a robot. The spaceship was empty. They were all alone!

'Why did everybody leave?' asked Kai.

'And why did they forget us?' asked Billy.

Nina thought about her parents. She couldn't understand it!

They decided to go back to the Control Room. Billy pressed lots of buttons and turned lots of dials. But nothing happened.

'We haven't got any power. And there's no contact with the Earth or the Lunar Recycling Plant.'

'So where is everybody?' asked Kai.

'I think there's only one answer,' Billy replied. The friends looked out of a window at the distant Moon.

'What do you think we should do?' asked Nina.

'We don't have any choice,' said Billy. 'We have to get down there to find help. We have to go to the Moon.'

STORY On the Dark Side of the Moon

Episode 4 ● 3.27

On the Moon

The Moon was a grey desert. It was dark, silent and still. There were only rocks, dust and craters. But a million stars were shining in the black sky.

One of the stars was moving. It was brighter than the other stars and closer to the surface of the Moon. And it was moving faster and faster across the sky ... But no, it wasn't a star. It was a small vehicle, a module from space station *Alastor*.

It was getting nearer to the surface of the Moon. And it was going too fast.

Inside the module, the friends were worried.

'What's happening, Billy?' asked Kai.

'I don't know!' shouted Billy. 'There's something wrong. I can't slow down the module!'

'Have you checked the engines?'

'I've already done that! I've tried everything.'

'So what can we do?'

'I'm going to try and land,' said Billy. 'It's going to be a bit uncomfortable. Get ready!'

They saw the Moon getting closer and closer. They were flying towards a huge rock. They were going to crash! Then Billy turned the controls ... and they flew over the top! But now they were going down into a huge crater.

'Here we go!' Billy shouted.

Nina closed her eyes. The module bounced like a ball! They went up ... and came down again ... and finally stopped.

'Is everybody OK?' Billy asked after a few seconds.

'I think so,' said Kai.

Nina opened her eyes and looked at Billy and Kai. Her body hurt in lots of different places. She tried to smile.

Five minutes later, the three friends stood on the Moon. They were wearing silver space suits.

'We were going towards the Recycling Plant when we crashed,' said Billy. 'It's over there. Let's go.'

After about an hour they reached the other side of the crater. Now they had to climb out. When they finally got to the top, Kai laughed happily. A Lunar Truck was only 100 metres away!

'We're going to be all right!' said Kai.

'Wait!' said Billy. 'Come with me.'

They moved behind a rock. Kai and Nina looked at him, confused.

Billy spoke quietly. 'I think something's wrong.'

STORY | On the Dark Side of the Moon

Episode 5 ● 3.28

Robots

The door of the Lunar Truck opened and two robots jumped out. These weren't normal robots. They were made of strange pieces of plastic and metal. One of them had three eyes, the other one had only one arm. In his one hand he was carrying a gun. And robots never carried guns!

'What are those weird robots?' asked Nina.

Kai shook his head. 'I don't know. I've never seen robots like them before. And I don't like them.'

Then the robots started speaking. But they weren't just speaking. They were arguing. And robots never argued!

'I saw something crash in the crater,' said Three Eyes.

'Don't be silly!' said One Arm. 'You always invent things!'

'I'm telling you, I saw something!'

'All right then. I'm going to look for it. And when I find it, I'm going to use this!' One Arm waved his gun in front of him. 'You can wait here.'

'I don't want to wait here on my own,' said Three Eyes.

'You're scared.'

'I'm not scared! I'm stressed out!'

'OK, come with me.'

The robots started walking towards the crater ... and towards Nina, Billy and Kai.

'If they see us, we'll be in big trouble,' said Kai.

Then One Arm pointed to the left.

'It's easier to get down over there,' he said.

'OK. Let's go that way,' replied Three Eyes. And they walked away.

Kai, Nina and Billy waited. When they couldn't see the robots, they climbed out of the crater and ran to the Lunar Truck. They sat down in the seats. Billy studied the controls.

'Do you know how to drive this thing?' asked Nina.

Billy smiled. He started the engine, released the brake ... and the Lunar Truck moved away.

Half an hour later, they saw enormous machines and ugly holes in the landscape. These were the holes where the Recycling Plant buried the rubbish from the Earth. Then they saw the three blue domes of the Recycling Plant. Another strange robot was standing at the entrance. Fortunately, it didn't look at them. It just pointed at the smallest dome. The friends drove towards it. Then they got out of the truck and entered the dome. They couldn't believe their eyes. There were hundreds of the weird robots standing in rows. Fortunately, they weren't moving.

'Let's take a look at them,' said Billy.

They were walking towards the robots when they heard voices.

'Quick, hide!' said Kai.

They ran behind a pile of metal and plastic rubbish. Then they saw a man with one of the weird robots. The man was tall with a short dark beard and a moustache. The robot had a round plastic clock for a face.

'That's Doctor Leon,' said Billy. 'I saw him about three months ago when he visited the *Alastor*. He's the man who's in charge of the Recycling Plant. And he's working with the robots!'

Episode 6 🔵 3.29

The prisoner

Doctor Leon walked up and down, examining the rows of robots.

'When can we begin?' asked Doctor Leon.

'In three hours,' said Clock Face.

'Are the humans safe?' he asked.

'Yes, Doctor Leon,' the robot replied. 'They are all sleeping.'

'Excellent. Then in three hours my Plastic Pirates will come alive. And the humans …'

Doctor Leon looked at Clock Face and laughed.

Nina looked nervously at Billy and Kai.

'What does he mean? Who are the humans?' she asked.

'I guess he means all the people from the *Alastor*,' Kai said slowly. 'My parents, your parents … .'

'But what's he going to do to them?'

'Sshh!' said Billy. 'He'll hear you.'

'Let's go and check out the humans,' said Doctor Leon. 'I can say goodbye to them.'

But before he could leave, two robots ran into the dome. It was Three Eyes and One Arm!

'What is it?' asked Doctor Leon. Three Eyes told him about the module. One Arm told him there was another human being on the Moon. 'And that human stole our Lunar Truck!' he said.

'I don't believe it!' said Doctor Leon angrily. 'How did that happen?'

'It was his fault!' said One Arm, pointing at Three Eyes.

'No, it wasn't! It was his fault!' said Three Eyes.

'Be quiet!' Doctor Leon shouted.

The robots stopped talking.

'We must find that human,' Doctor Leon said. And then he added with a smile, 'We can put him with the others.'

Nina was scared. Very scared. She took a step backwards … and she touched some rubbish. A dirty metal ball fell noisily to the ground. She watched it roll and slowly come to a stop. Billy and Kai looked at her in horror.

'What was that?' asked Doctor Leon. He stared at the pile of rubbish where the friends were hiding. 'Go and look!' he said to his robots.

'They're going to find us,' said Kai.

'I'm so sorry,' said Nina.

They heard the robots getting closer.

'What are we going to do?' she asked.

'Don't worry,' said Kai. 'It will be all right.'

He smiled … and then he started running. Nina couldn't stop him. Kai ran around the pile shouting and waving his arms. The robots chased him.

'I've caught him!' said Three Eyes.

'No, I've caught him!' said One Arm.

They were both right. Kai was a prisoner!

Episode 7 3.30

Doctor Leon's plan

'He's just a silly little boy!' said Doctor Leon. Three Eyes, One Arm and Clock Face laughed.

Kai didn't laugh. 'What's going on? What happened to everybody on the *Alastor*?'

'Do you want to see them?' Doctor Leon asked. 'Come this way.'

They walked over to two large doors in the side of the dome. Clock Face opened them and Kai saw a large dark room. In the darkness he saw people. They were lying on the floor. Their eyes were closed. Then Kai saw his mother's face ...

'What have you done to them?' he screamed.

'Oh, don't worry about them,' Doctor Leon said. 'They're only sleeping. I gave them the same drug that I used on your space station.

But I have plans for them.'

Doctor Leon waved a hand at the lines of silent robots.

'Do you like my robots? Normal robots are so boring. They have to obey people. They're so polite! But I can give my robots life. I can make them think and feel!'

'How can you do that?' asked Kai.

'I can't actually create real brains. But I can steal the thoughts of real people and put them in the brains of my robots. And then my Plastic Robots will live! I'll have the biggest and the most powerful gang of Space Pirates. And I'll become rich!'

'But what about the people?' asked Kai. Doctor Leon looked at Kai and smiled.

Nina and Billy were listening to the conversation when Nina saw something.

'Hey, look over there. That's Charles!' she said quietly.

Charles was standing behind a large machine. He was watching Kai and Doctor Leon.

'He looks worried,' she said.

'Don't be silly,' said Billy. 'Robots don't have feelings.'

Nina didn't answer. She took a decision. She found a plastic ball in the rubbish and rolled it towards Charles.

'Are you mad?' said Billy, watching the ball. 'Can we trust him?'

'Of course we can trust him,' said Nina.

Nina was great at ball games. The plastic ball hit Charles's foot! The robot looked down at the ball, then turned towards her. He paused, then walked quickly towards them.

Charles looked at Nina and Kai. 'Hello,' he said.

'Hello, Charles,' said Nina. 'Are you all right?'

'I'm fine, thank you,' said Charles.

'Where are the other robots from the *Alastor*?'

'Well, Doctor Leon brought us all here with the humans. But I escaped and hid. Unfortunately, the other robots are ...' He stopped for a moment, then continued. 'Doctor Leon put them in the recycling machines. And that is where he is going to put the people – after he has taken their brains.'

Nina put her hand to her mouth.

'We have to wake them up,' said Charles.

'How can we do that?' asked Billy.

Episode 8 3.31

Charles to the rescue!

'I found this cylinder in Doctor Leon's laboratory,' explained Charles. 'It contains a special gas. It will wake up the people. But first I have to get to that room. And it's very difficult.'

But then his voice suddenly sounded stronger.

'I have an idea,' he said.

Charles took some bits of plastic rubbish – knives and plates and toys – and fixed them to his head and body. He whispered some instructions to Billy and Nina. Then he left them.

Charles walked quickly, waving his arms.

'Doctor Leon! Doctor Leon!'

'What is it?' asked Doctor Leon, surprised. 'What's happening?'

'I've just come from outside,' said Charles. 'Other modules have landed. The Recycling Plant is surrounded by humans!'

'Humans? Where have they come from?'

'From the Alastor!'

'That's impossible!' screamed Doctor Leon. 'My robots captured everybody ...'

Kai was staring at the new robot in amazement. He knew who it was!

'Your robots didn't capture me,' Kai said. 'And they didn't catch lots of other people, too!'

'The humans are coming NOW!' shouted Charles.

Nina and Billy started throwing lots of pieces of metal at Doctor Leon and his robots. Kai quickly jumped out of the way.

One Arm was hit on the head and fell to the floor.

Clock Face tried to run away and fell over One Arm.

Three Eyes tried to hide behind Doctor Leon.

And Charles ran towards the door in the wall. He opened the metal cylinder and threw it into the room.

Doctor Leon looked around the dome.

'I don't believe it! Where are the other humans?' he screamed. 'Where are they?'

'Here they are!' shouted Charles. And the people from the room walked into the dome. They were awake again – and safe!

'And don't forget us!' said a girl's voice.

Doctor Leon looked round and saw Nina and Billy.

'I don't believe it,' he said. 'I was beaten by three kids and a silly robot!'

At this moment, Three Eyes tried to escape. He ran through one of the doors. Unfortunately, it was the entrance to the Recycling Plant. And in 30 seconds, he was recycled!

The people from the Alastor made a circle around Doctor Leon.

'Doctor Leon,' said Charles. 'I'm afraid you have lost.'

Twenty-four hours later, Nina, Kai and Billy were hanging out in their secret room. But they weren't alone. Charles was with them. And they were listening to Rihanna. The music was over 100 years old.

'Do you like this music, Charles?' asked Nina.

'It's interesting,' said Charles.

'And are you happy to be back on the Alastor?' asked Kai.

'I really can't answer that question,' said Charles. 'You know, I don't have any feelings. But if I had feelings, I would be happy.'

'Charles,' said Kai, smiling, 'I think your answer means "yes".'

And everybody laughed – except Charles, of course!

Unit 1

1 Complete the sentences with the past simple.

1 My little sister ....*ate*........ too much ice cream at the party. (eat)

2 My brother .... a new car last week. (buy)

3 I .... this really good book in the library. (find)

4 Why .... you .... the TV? (turn off)

5 .... you .... to the supermarket yesterday? (go)

6 Alfie .... his new trainers to school. (not wear)

2 (Circle) the correct answer.

1 She .... eating her breakfast while she was doing her Maths homework.
   a (was) b is c were

2 When the accident ...., was the driver talking on his mobile?
   a was happening b happened c happens

3 While they .... they saw an octopus.
   a were swimming b swam c was swimming

4 You .... your laptop when a plane is taking off.
   a must use b mustn't use c don't have to use

5 I .... my homework before dinner because I watch TV after.
   a don't have to b have to do c must to do

6 Hurrah! We .... to school tomorrow – it's a holiday.
   a don't have to go b must go c mustn't go

3 🔊 1.08 Listen and complete the text.

Last February I ¹ ....*went*.... to the famous Venice carnival. We arrived at the station in the morning and ² .... a water bus to St Mark's Square. While we ³ .... on the water bus we ⁴ .... hundreds of people in fantastic costumes. I ⁵ .... lots of photos. We ⁶ .... walk on the left side of the narrow streets because they were so crowded! While we ⁷ .... a procession we ⁸ .... an old friend, so we went to a café and ⁹ .... a hot chocolate together. At six o'clock we ¹⁰ .... back to the station and got a train home.

Unit 2

1 Put the words in the correct order to make sentences.

1 tomorrow / it / will / snow / morning / ?
   Will it snow tomorrow morning?

2 Maths / my / won't / I / pass / test

3 2100 / the / on / live / people / Moon / will / in / ?

4 your / come / party / Lucy / to / will / ?

5 to / students / go / will / university / many

6 of / give / the / will / teacher / us / lots / homework / ?

2 (Circle) the correct answer.

1 **Waiter** What would you like?
   Customer .... a hamburger and chips, please.
   a I'm having b (I'll have) c I have

2 Jamie and I .... tennis at three o'clock tomorrow.
   a are playing b will play c play

3 Watch out! That bottle .... on the floor.
   a is going to fall b will fall c falls

4 We .... our homework again. We promise.
   a won't forget b aren't forgetting c forget

5 I think that next year I .... to surf.
   a am going to learn b am learning c learn

6 What are you .... at the weekend?
   a to do b doing c will do

3 🔊 1.18 Listen and complete the text.

<u>My city in 2050 by Jodie</u>

I think that my city ¹ ....*will have*.... less traffic in 2050 and it will be quieter. There ² .... flying cars and they will run on electricity. Buildings will be very tall and they ³ .... green roofs, and people will grow vegetables on them. We will use rain water in our homes. Electricity ⁴ .... from the Sun and wind power. All schools will have computers, and there ⁵ .... many teachers because we will have digital lessons. We ⁶ .... cars very often because we ⁷ .... bikes. There will be lots of cycle paths. Lots of people ⁸ .... at home and have video meetings. Restaurants and shops will have robot waiters and assistants. Some people from my city ⁹ .... and ¹⁰ .... in space stations.

Unit 3

1 Complete the sentences with *for* or *since*.

1 We've been in this room __since__ nine o'clock this morning.
2 They've lived in Los Angeles _____ 2007.
3 I've had this watch _____ three months.
4 Katie has known Olivia _____ last year.
5 You've had my dictionary _____ last Tuesday. Can I have it back?
6 He's played for Manchester United _____ two years.

2 (Circle) the correct answer.

1 Have you ever eaten Chinese food? **(Yes, I have.)** / **Yes, I have eaten.**
2 I've been to Disneyland. I **have been** / **went** there last year.
3 Adriana **saw** / **has seen** that film last week. She doesn't want to see it again.
4 I've **ever** / **never** been to Australia. It's too far.
5 I'm hungry! I **didn't eat** / **haven't eaten** today.
6 **Did you do** / **Have you done** your homework last night?
7 Have you ever **ridden** / **rode** a horse? No, I haven't.
8 I can't believe it! My best friend **has never seen** / **did never see** a rainbow.
9 Where's your dad? Has he **been** / **gone** shopping?
10 Have you **never** / **ever** been to Paris?

3 🔊 1.29 Listen and complete the text.

Ronaldinho is one of the world's most famous footballers. He ¹ __has played__ football since he was a little boy. He was born in 1980 in Brazil and his family ² _____ crazy about football. Sadly, his father died when Ronaldinho ³ _____ only eight years old. Ronaldinho ⁴ _____ football and joined a football school. When he was 13 he ⁵ _____ all 23 goals against a local team! He ⁶ _____ a professional when he was 17. Ronaldinho ⁷ _____ a very interesting life and ⁸ _____ many countries. He ⁹ _____ for different teams in his life including Paris Saint-Germain and FC Barcelona and, of course, Brazil! He ¹⁰ _____ a Spanish citizen in 2007.

Unit 4

1 Complete the sentences with *already*, *just* or *yet*.

1 **Naomi** I like your new T-shirt! It's cool.
  Dan Thanks, I've __just__ bought it.
2 **Teacher** Where's your homework?
  Luka I haven't done it _____ .
3 **Ella** What about page 30?
  Teacher We've _____ done it. We did it last lesson.
4 **Mum** I've _____ had a phone call from Grace in Canada.
  Dad Great. How is she?
5 **Kate** Oh, no! We haven't got anything for dinner.
  Adam Relax! I've _____ bought everything we need.
6 **Alicia** How are your diving lessons going?
  Pablo Not bad. But I haven't learnt to dive off the high board _____ .

2 (Circle) the correct indefinite pronoun.

1 I've lost my glasses. I think they are **anywhere** / **(somewhere)** in the living room.
2 Come here. I want to tell you **something** / **somebody**.
3 **Nobody** / **Nothing** comes to the extra Maths class, so the teacher has cancelled it.
4 It's good. There is recycling **nowhere** / **everywhere** in my town.
5 Listen! There's **nobody** / **somebody** at the door. Go and open it.
6 I'm so bored. There's **anything** / **nothing** to do.

3 🔊 1.37 Listen and complete the text.

I go to ballet school. I want to be a professional dancer. It's hard work but fun at my school. ¹ __Everybody__ has ballet lessons in the morning and then we do normal classes during the school day. I think we have ² _____ classes, but I enjoy them! I think we have ³ _____ pressure sometimes. When we do shows we often have ⁴ _____ dances to learn. Plus I have homework in the evening. So usually I've just got ⁵ _____ to do! I practise every night and I ⁶ _____ always get ⁷ _____ sleep. And I ⁸ _____ really have ⁹ _____ time to see my friends either. But I wouldn't swap my life with ¹⁰ _____ !

Unit 5

1 Complete the sentences with the correct form of the verbs in brackets.

1 We ____will walk____ to school if it ____snows____ tomorrow. (walk / snow)
2 If you _____ America, _____ to New York? (visit / you go)
3 If you _____ blue and yellow, you _____ green. (mix / make)
4 If they _____ the late night film, they _____ tired tomorrow. (watch / be)
5 If your cousins _____ to stay for New Year, _____ them to our party? (come / you invite)
6 I _____ these new words if I _____. (not learn / not concentrate)
7 If you _____ an accident, _____ the police. (see / call)
8 If your mum _____ angry, we _____ tonight. (be / not go out)

2 (Circle) the correct answer.

1 I know a shop ____which____ sells iguanas.
   a who   b (which)   c where
2 I like the actor _____ starred in the last James Bond film.
   a who   b which   c where
3 I wore those designer jeans _____ I bought on Saturday.
   a who   b which   c where
4 We visited the street _____ Scarlett Johansson lives.
   a who   b which   c where
5 That's the shop assistant _____ helped me.
   a who   b which   c where

3 ⊙ 2.08 Listen and complete the text.

I live in a city [1] ____that____ is famous for its ancient university – Cambridge. I am going to a football match at the weekend with George and Joe, [2] _____ are my best friends. It's in Abbey stadium [3] _____ Cambridge plays home matches. The match [4] _____ we are going to watch is Cambridge United against Stevenage. George and I are fans of Cambridge United, but Joe is a Chelsea fan. He prefers footballers [5] _____ play for bigger teams. He says they play better football, but we prefer our local team! If our team [6] _____, we [7] _____ really happy. But if they [8] _____ we [9] _____ too upset. It's still fun!

Unit 6

1 Write sentences using reported speech.

1 'I want to go to bed.'
   David said ____he wanted to go to bed.____
2 'We're going to the cinema on Tuesday.'
   Maria said _____
3 'It's going to rain.'
   Freddie said _____
4 'I'm writing a script for a film.'
   Sofia said _____
5 'My brother hates getting up early.'
   Grace said _____
6 'I must visit my grandparents.'
   Aydin said _____

2 (Circle) the correct answer.

1 They (said) / told / asked they were sorry they were late.
2 I said / told / asked Luke if he was feeling better today.
3 Ryan said / told / asked me he was thirsty.
4 Kyle said / told / asked he was going to buy the tickets on Monday.
5 Layla said / told / asked Ryan she didn't like football very much.
6 Josh said / told / asked his parents he wasn't hungry.

3 ⊙ 2.23 Listen and complete the text.

I love going to the cinema. Last week, I [1] ____asked____ my friend Jake if he [2] _____ Johnny Depp films. He told [3] _____ he loved them. So I asked him [4] _____ he wanted to see his latest film. Jake said he did. I said we [5] _____ meet outside the cinema at six-thirty on Saturday. Three days later, I was [6] _____ outside the cinema in the rain. It was quarter to seven and I was waiting for Jake. I called him on my mobile and I asked if he [7] _____ feeling OK. Jake [8] _____ he was feeling fine. Then I asked if he was coming to the cinema. He [9] _____ me he was, just as we agreed, on Sunday. I like Jake a lot but he never listens! In the end I [10] _____ the film on my own. It was great!

Unit 7

1 Complete the sentences with _a little_ or _a few_.

1 I speak _a little_ Arabic.
2 There are .... biscuits in the packet. Would you like one?
3 I found .... information on the internet.
4 There's only .... sugar, so we can't make a cake.
5 Only .... students came to the extra lesson yesterday.
6 Quick! My bus leaves in .... minutes.

2 Circle the correct answer.

1 If I .... a scooter, I'd ride it to school.
   a had b would have c have
2 I .... Science if I went to university.
   a study b would study c have studied
3 What .... life be like if there were no electricity?
   a will b is c would
4 If we .... a dog, I wouldn't go to the park so often.
   a not have b didn't have c wouldn't have
5 What would you do if you .... a lot of money?
   a find b found c would find
6 If my sister were older, she .... so naughty.
   a isn't b wasn't c wouldn't be

3 ⊙ 2.34 Listen and complete the text.

My dream

Hi, my name's Amelia. My dream is to learn to fly and become an airline pilot. If I ¹ _were_ an airline pilot, I would ² .... around the world and see wonderful places. I ³ .... train for a long time, and I would ⁴ .... a lot of responsibility. If I ⁵ .... a pilot, I would ⁶ .... a very smart uniform and a hat, and I ⁷ .... carry a special bag. Pilots talk to their passengers and tell them about the places they are flying over. I ⁸ .... enjoy that. I would ⁹ .... the same things every day, but I ¹⁰ .... get bored. My ambition is to become a captain.

Unit 8

1 Circle the correct answer.

1 This chocolate _is made_ in Switzerland.
   a made b is made
2 Who .... the aeroplane?
   a invented b was invented
3 Mozart .... a lot of music.
   a was composed b composed
4 Sara .... all her friends to the party.
   a invited b was invited
5 Britain .... by the ancient Romans.
   a invaded b was invaded
6 We .... lots of homework by our teacher.
   a give b are given

2 Complete the sentences with the passive form of the verbs in brackets.

1 Tennis _is played_ at Wimbledon in London. (play)
2 The _Mona Lisa_ _was painted_ by Leonardo da Vinci. (paint)
3 Tea .... in England. (not grow)
4 _Hamlet_ .... by Shakespeare. (write)
5 The Statue of Liberty .... in France, not the USA. (build)
6 _The Lord of the Rings_ .... in New Zealand. (film)

3 ⊙ 3.02 Listen and complete the text.

The Notting Hill Carnival is Europe's biggest street festival. It takes place in London in the last weekend of August and it ¹ _is visited_ by over a million visitors from all around the world! The roads ² .... in the area and loud music ³ .... from lots of big sound systems. ⁴ .... amazing parades and colourful costumes ⁵ .... by the dancers and musicians. Typical Caribbean food ⁶ .... from hundreds of stalls. On Sunday prizes ⁷ .... to children for their costumes and on Monday the main parade ⁸ .... The first carnival ⁹ .... in 1966 – it was very small. Now the carnival ¹⁰ .... months in advance!

Unit 9

1 **Complete the sentences with the correct question tag.**

1 You like playing chess, _don't you_ ?
2 Your sister composes music, ... ?
3 Eric can speak three languages, ... ?
4 We haven't got any lessons tomorrow, ... ?
5 They're travelling by plane, ... ?
6 Science is quite difficult, ... ?

2 (Circle) **the correct option.**

1 .... broke this window?
  a Where **b** (Who)
2 Which film .... at the cinema?
  a saw you **b** did you see
3 .... did you travel to Argentina?
  a Where **b** How
4 .... did you see this morning?
  a Who **b** Why
5 When .... for the first time?
  a did you meet **b** met you
6 Who .... that text message?
  a sent **b** did send

3 🔘 **3.12 Listen and complete the text.**

My brother James is clever but he isn't very confident. I was drinking some juice in the kitchen when he came in with his homework.
'You've got some time to help me with my homework, ¹ _haven't_ you?' he asked.
'Yes, I ² ....,' I said.
'³ .... can I help?'
'I just want to check some things with you,' he said. 'Oscar Wilde wrote stories and plays, ⁴ .... he?' James said.
'Yes, he ⁵ ....,' I said.
'There are 50 American states, ⁶ .... there?' he said.
'Yes, I think so.'
'And monkeys can swim, ⁷ .... they?' he said.
'Yes, they ⁸ ....,' I said.
'But ⁹ .... invented the first computer?' he asked.
'I don't know,' I said. '¹⁰ .... don't you find out on your computer!'

Unit 10

1 **Complete the sentences with the correct form of *used to*.**

1 My mother _used to_ live in a small village.
2 I .... read novels, but I love them now.
3 .... you .... have lots of toys?
4 Alfie .... eat too much junk food, but now he eats healthy food.
5 My grandparents .... have a computer, but now they can't live without one!
6 Where .... they .... live?

2 (Circle) **the correct option.**

1 I .... many films this year.
  a (haven't seen) **b** didn't see
2 He asked if there .... anything to eat.
  a is **b** was
3 You won't eat your dinner if you .... any more biscuits.
  a have **b** will have
4 Olivia .... swimming three times last week.
  a went **b** have been
5 Have you done your homework .... ?
  a already **b** yet
6 If I .... a bear, I'd be really scared!
  a I'd see **b** saw

3 🔘 **3.20 Listen and complete the text.**

My grandmother ¹ _told_ me about her childhood yesterday. When she was a girl, she ² .... to live in the country. Her parents used to ³ .... a cottage in a forest. My grandmother ⁴ .... the cottage was small but it was really beautiful. They didn't ⁵ .... to have central heating. There was a wood fire in every room. She ⁶ .... that sometimes in the morning there was ice on the inside of the windows! They ⁷ .... use to have a car. They ⁸ .... to have a horse and cart and they went everywhere on that. I ⁹ .... that a horse and cart was very romantic. She said it ¹⁰ .... very uncomfortable!

Your Space Web Zone

http://yourspace.cambridge.org

Your Space DVD

Featuring:

Video diaries

Viewpoints

Communication

Culture

CLIL

Surprise your teens!

These fabulous activities are
sure to get them involved.
Just photocopy and go!

CAMBRIDGE English Language Teaching

Choose YOUR story

The readers series for teenagers

stimulating

Thrilling
Breathtaking

Exciting

Amazing Young Sports People
Mandy Loader

Gone!
Margaret Johnson

Killer Bees
Jane Rollason

Cambridge
Discovery
Readers

w.cambridge.org/elt/discoveryreaders

CAMBRIDGE
UNIVERSITY PRESS